T0114195

Paris Demystified

Making the Most of Your Paris Visit

Sarah C. Dorr and Richard S. Dorr

Order this book online at www.trafford.com
or email orders@trafford.com

Most Trafford titles are also available at major online book retailers.

The artwork on the cover of many Paris guidebooks would depict the most famous Paris icons.
Reflecting the more selective, personal nature of this book, Catherine E. Clark's artwork
on the cover displays six elements of the authors' own "personal sanctuary" in the City of
Light. Reading clockwise, and beginning with the upper left-handed image: A café located
in the 5th Arrondissement; a windmill on Montmartre; a hotel in the 7th Arrondissement;
Shakespeare & Company bookstore; a café in the 7th Arrondissement; and l'Opéra Garnier.

The authors have made every effort to ensure the accuracy of the information in this
book at the time of going to press. However they cannot take responsibility for any
loss, injury of inconvenience resulting from information contained therein.

Printed in the United States of America.

ISBN: 978-1-4251-1641-5 (sc)

Trafford rev. 11/29/2010

 www.trafford.com

North America & international
toll-free: 1 888 232 4444 (USA & Canada)
phone: 250 383 6864 ♦ fax: 812 355 4082

Dedicated to Sylvia Beach,
George Whitman, and Sylvia Beach Whitman
Spiritual Shepherds of the Literary Flock
in the City of Enlightenment

Contents

Contents (Continued)

Foreword

Considering a trip to Paris? Maybe it's your first. Or your Parisian appetite may have been whetted by previous exposure. In either case, Paris—though magical—can be daunting. Confronting language differences, haphazard street patterns, unfamiliar local attitudes, transportation quandaries, safety hazards, and the sheer number of sightseeing and dining alternatives can be overwhelming, frustrating and draining. Too often, the result is sapped vitality that inhibits the visitor from getting the most out of Paris due to tacit acceptance of what might be termed "Paris by default"—making decisions based primarily on what's expedient, popular, easily accessible or energy-conserving.

We're a husband and wife team from the U.S. East Coast. More than a quarter century ago, Sally suggested a post-honeymoon trip to Paris. Dick quivered in his loafers as he recalled that his landmark high school French achievement involved surreptitiously sneaking sandwiches in class. But, reasoning that the honeymoon was over and couldn't be ruined at that point, we went. And we went.....bonkers!!

Over many revisits, Paris has become a treasured haven for us—but not without numerous trials and assorted tribulations. Every trip has taught us valuable lessons—which leads us to the unique niche of this book, written *for* tourists *by* veteran Paris tourists.

There's no way you're going to experience every facet of Paris during one, two, or even ten visits. It's prudent to prepare for each visit with a strategic "plan of attack" to ensure that, by the end of your trip, you've sampled a thorough cross-section of the City of Light while accommodating your time frame and your budget.

Traditional guidebooks contain overwhelming masses of information and detail. But, unlike a typical guidebook, *Paris Demystified focuses on guiding you as you customize your strategic plan, set your priorities, and maximize the efficiency of your visit.* Use this book to develop your strategic plan; and then consider referring to standard guidebooks to supplement the many details we have provided.

3

Optimizing Your Time for Enjoying Paris

If you're a first-timer, what are your most pressing concerns after your plane lands? (No, we mean *besides* finding a "toilette.") Our guess is that you're anxious to surmount often-daunting logistical barriers so you may "hit the ground running" and maximize the time you spend enjoying yourself. We've developed an innovative series of strategies toward that end, with an emphasis on avoiding time-consuming pitfalls as you become comfortable with the logistics of Paris.

• We'll go into detail about when to take your trip, how to choose a hotel, what to pack, negotiating the airport, alternatives for getting into the city, quickly familiarizing yourself with Paris, dealing with currency exchange, short cuts to coping with language differences, efficiently planning your sightseeing, avoiding petty theft, and more.

• You'll find overviews of 70+ major attractions with addresses, hours of operation, nearest Métro stops, and phone numbers. Sift through them; decide which ones appeal to you; and refer to a conventional guide book to supplement what we say about them. We've also developed several half-day, geographically clustered sightseeing modules combining popular and "under the radar" attractions.

• One of our goals is to introduce simplicity to situations that can lead to confusion and fatigue. On our first Paris trip, Dick insisted on making the restaurant reservations and dealing with taxi drivers in his very tentative French. Much of what he said (or thought he was saying) wasn't understood—especially our name. We realized it made sense to *spell* confusing words. So we scoured guidebooks for a phonetic French alphabet. Proving unsuccessful, we have since created our own. It will prove helpful in making dinner reservations, giving street names to taxi drivers, introducing yourself, etc.

By the way, Dick continues to practice his *slowly* improving French by making most of our arrangements in Paris. Sometimes, he and his stubborn streak encounter an equally obstinate Parisian who's determined to try out his or her English; and the two tenaciously carry on a bizarre conversation in each other's language.

4

- On the subject of language, we've identified 40 "French survival" terms that the Paris visitor should know in order to get by quite nicely (and be received more warmly) in Paris—where an attempt in halting French is usually preferable to no French at all. We'll list these 40 terms, with phonetic pronunciations; and you'll be gratified to find that you already know at least half of them. While phonetic pronunciations will also be provided for more than an additional 300 travel-helpful words and phrases, it's the 40 survival terms that you most need to deposit in the old memory bank.

- The Paris Métro is an exceptional subway and a lifesaver for the weary of foot. The conventional method of identifying destinations and connections among Métro lines necessitates deciphering a Métro map. Trying to unravel the criss-crossing lines (displayed in various colors, some of which are maddeningly similar to one another) can be the essence of frustration—especially out in the rain. We've compiled an easy-to-use *list* of Métro stations and connections that simplifies matters dramatically.

- The Paris dining-out experience typically commences with the "interrogation cadence" a maître d' uses to take reservations— day, time, number in the party, name, etc. You'll often receive more cordial treatment (and sometimes better seating) if you try it in French—and some proprietors of small restaurants don't speak English anyway. We'll provide a detailed *script* (with phonetic French pronunciations) for you to follow in making reservations.

- Paris is similar to any large city in terms of the possibility of petty theft. Parisian pickpockets are batting zero in four attempts against us. Rather than issuing the usual banal warning to be careful, we'll provide details on how and where petty thieves typically go about their dirty work—as well as how to stump them.

Paris Immersion

Paris Demystified will guide you in doing and seeing as much as possible in Paris without becoming overly fatigued.

- In addition to our previously mentioned sightseeing modules, we'll offer frequently passionate opinions on attractions, restaurants, drinking spots, people-watching perches, and panoramic scenic vistas we feel are particularly deserving of your attention—and why.

- Information on popular attractions such as Notre Dame and the Louvre are in any guidebook. We'll certainly address them, but we'll emphasize selected, special "under the radar" attractions. You'll learn why, despite the fact that we revere all of Paris' icons, we prefer Ste.-Chappelle over Notre Dame and Musée d'Orsay over the Louvre. We hope you'll see all of them, but maybe we can give you something to think about when it comes to time allocation.

Bonding with Paris

We believe each visitor who gets caught up in the Paris mystique forms a very personal and unique series of attachments with Paris that collectively epitomize what Paris symbolizes to him or her. A park here; a café there; a special sightseeing vista; a boutique; a people-watching vantage point; a favorite crêpe stand; a special bookstore; a monument; a human relationship. The possibilities are nearly endless.

We regard the collective core of our intimate attachment to Paris as a form of unique *personal sanctuary* to which we may privately retreat in our minds, even when we're geographically removed. The notion of personal sanctuary intensifies with each visit, as one's experiences expand from a focus on sightseeing and dining to greater appreciation of the flow and rhythms of ordinary Parisian life,

A detailed strategy will be offered for forming your own personal sanctuary, while encountering unexpected adventures and identifying practical resources along the way. We'll also relate a number of our own experiences as examples of how this philosophy works.

The pseudonym for Paris is the *City of Light*—NOT the City of Light**S**. While Paris does feature brilliant lighting, it is the inner glow of *personal enlightenment* that most typifies the city's unique charm. In this jewel of a metropolis, we are infused by feelings of well-being. In fact, each of us has elected Paris as the place to recuperate from major medical procedures.

People ask us what's so special about Paris. We've discussed this query over many pleasant glasses of wine. Is it the spectacular vistas? The fascinating people-watching? The legendary cuisine? The fashion sense? The monumental icons? The aura of timelessness? The outdoor markets? The storied museums? The idyllic parks? The classic architecture? The café life? The romantic strolls? The poetry of the language? The energy the city exudes? To some extent, it's a confluence of all of the above.

But our powerful bond to Paris is, first and foremost, a function of *the kinds of people we become* when in Paris. We observe and find ourselves reflective. We explore, and our senses are heightened. We discover and are uplifted. We dream and find ourselves transported. As Gene Kelly's *Jerry Mulligan* says in the movie, *An American in Paris*, "It's too real and too beautiful to ever let you forget anything." Notwithstanding the split infinitive, he has a point.

In compiling the book, we've ventured well beyond our own experiences. Commentary from returning Paris visitors has been a significant catalyst. Too often, we've cringed at disquieting reports:

"There I was at the airport without a clue."
"The street layout makes no sense."
"Empty taxis wouldn't stop when I hailed them."
"Parisians are snobs!"
"I felt like a jerk making dinner reservations."
"I found the sightseeing to be exhausting."
"When I exchanged dollars for euros, I thought I was being robbed!"
"My hair dryer exploded!"
"I was constantly worried about pickpockets."

7

As much as such reviews dishearten us, the frustration they bespeak has provided an important forum for our book. Using investigative skills honed in our careers as researchers, we've supplemented our own perspectives by scouring hundreds of books, newsletters, websites, personal recommendations, and other resources. We've also obtained inputs from a number of Parisians.

In fact, we've consulted tourists and Parisians alike to examine the reputation of the French for aloofness and arrogance. Heeding our in-depth tips for understanding and dealing with denizens of the French Capital will be a reassuring source of comfort as you bond with Paris.

For some readers, this book may infuse a practical sense of reassurance in dealing with Paris and Parisians. Others may find their previous Parisian horizons broadened. Whatever your situation, our ultimate objective is to help you avoid "Paris by default" and connect with Paris in ways that will usher you down the pathway to an enduring, passionate connection with this magnificent city.

We are beholden to the many kind souls who have waded through and utilized various drafts of this book while in Paris in order to provide candid critiques. The support of George Whitman, owner of the *Shakespeare & Company* English language bookstore in Paris, has been an inspiration—as have inputs from treasured Parisian friends like René, Thierry and their families.

Our Monday Club comrades deserve special recognition for their extended leap of faith in believing there really would be a book called *Paris Demystified*. A debt of gratitude goes out to our dear friends, Barbara and Steve (who must hold the record for critiquing the largest number of drafts of the book), and for the continuing support of Peg, Terry, Olga and Matt. We are particularly grateful to our good friend, Catherine E. Clark, whose artistry produced the beautiful pen-and-ink sketches that grace the front cover.

Paris can be as special for you as it is for us. We sincerely hope *Paris Demystified* will help to propel you in that direction; and we wish you "Bon Voyage."

A Seamless Arrival

It's easy to underestimate the importance of advance planning for a trip. Some leave it all to a travel agency. Depending on someone who knows the ropes can foster a legitimate sense of security.

But **don't** assume the tour professionals have done everything and all that remains is to grab the camera and start clicking. That attitude is a prelude to accepting what we call "Paris by default"—limiting yourself to the most popular and easily accessible touristy stuff.

What follows are some aids in planning the trip. Even veteran travelers or those who are using a tour professional would be well-advised to look through this book.

When to Go

The following chart contains our three weather priorities in determining what month to visit Paris—temperature range (average high and low); percentage of days with no precipitation; and average number of sunlight hours per day. National holidays are also shown.

| | Avg. Temp | | % of Days with No | Avg. hrs. | |
	Hi	Lo	Precip.	Daylight	Major Holidays
Jan.	43F	34F	45%	2/day	New Year's Day
Feb.	45F	34F	50%	3/day	
Mar.	51F	38F	47%	5/day	Easter Sunday (Mar. or
Apr.	57F	42F	50%	6/day	Easter Monday Apr.)
May	64F	49F	52%	10/day	May 1 (Labor), 8 (Victory Day) Ascension-Easter + 39 (May or
Jun.	70F	54F	57%	13/day	Pentecost-Easter + 49 June)
Jul.	75F	58F	65%	15/day	July 14 (Bastille Day)
Aug.	75F	57F	61%	14/day	Aug. 15 (Assumption)
Sep.	69F	52F	60%	12/day	
Oct.	59F	46F	55%	8/day	
Nov.	49F	39F	50%	5/day	Nov. 1 (All Saints' Day); 11 (Armistice Day)
Dec.	45F	36F	48%	2/day	Dec. 25 (Christmas)

Statistically, July and August appear the choicest months, ranking highest in all three categories. However, tourist glut can be a major problem during these two months. (Call us crazy, but we feel that we can see thousands of Americans at home for free.) Bastille Day (July 14, celebrating French independence) attracts hordes of people. Many Parisians flee the city in August, and numerous restaurants and some shops close for the entire month.

We prefer either May (if you're an enthusiast of spring vegetation) or the first two weeks of June, with September ranking a very close third. These time periods are usually temperate; daylight lasts until reasonably late in the evening. Tourism is well below its peak. And French families are at work or school.

Airline bargains may make April and October worthy of consideration, but be prepared for weather quirks. Airfare and hotels are least expensive during winter months, and the Christmas lights are beautiful; but November-March tend to be dark, damp, and cold.

If you visit Paris during a State holiday such as May 8th, July 14th or November 11th, the pageantry and parades can be impressive. But Paris holidays can be mentally and physically debilitating. The more major the holiday, the more streets may be closed, and you may walk far out of your way. The Métro is loaded and slow, and beleagured taxi drivers may take you anywhere except where you want to go.

One warning about the Métro. Parisians are famous for going on strike without notice—particularly transportation workers and especially around holidays. On numerous instances, a Métro train has stopped at a station and the operators have simply vanished, leaving passengers to disembark and fend for themselves. If you're "lucky," a strike may be announced in advance; and many last for only one day.

Tip: Get Métro tickets in advance of holidays; some smaller Métro stations do not sell them on holidays.

Tip: If a holiday falls on Tuesday or Thursday, a four-day weekend is usually observed. Shops and banks are generally closed.

What to Take

You'll feel more comfortable if your tourist persona is not incredibly conspicuous. Since you'll be seen by many more people than you'll speak with, your appearance is the number one way to stick out like a sore thumb. If you'd like to become the tourist poster child, wear shorts, a t-shirt, sneakers, a fanny pack, a baseball cap, or a béret. (Bérets have been "out" for years.)

Strive for comfort in your apparel planning. Parisians achieve their chic from tastefulness more than elegance. For example, decorative scarves are de rigueur among most Parisian women for "dressing up" outfits. This is a great city for walking, but don't try to break in new walking shoes. Apply water-repellent spray to the old klunkers, in which you'll spend much more time than you anticipated. For women, flats are great for dealing with slippery cobblestones; but make certain they have non-skid soles.

Tip: Versatility, washability, practicality and comfort should be the watchwords in planning your Parisian wardrobe.

Never were the concepts of "mix and match" and "layering" more appropriate. Basic black has been "in" for quite a while. For men, it's hard to go wrong with khakis or wool slacks and sport shirts during the day. Women will be comfortable with slacks and a wrinkle-proof blouse. Black jeans are okay, but blue jeans are usually worn by only the very young.

For evening dining at a nice restaurant, a man need only add a sport jacket to the aforementioned costume. (Go ahead, take it; you can always remove it.) Neckties are for only *very* upscale restaurants. A woman will feel comfortable in a pants suit, skirt or dress, depending on the prestige of the restaurant. Handbags should have shoulder straps for security purposes. Take a water-repellant windbreaker.

Tip: Consider taking a medium-length raincoat, preferably with removable lining if there's the possibility of cold weather. A versatile precaution against fickle weather, it will also conceal tempting pants pockets from thieves.

An umbrella in Paris is essential. If you have none, try discount stores such as the 30 Paris locations of Monoprix/Prixunic/Uniprix (telephone 01.40.75.11.02) or sidewalk displays on Rue de Rivoli.

Tip: Keep your passport, money, credit cards, and ATM cards in interior or closable pockets (or a hidden money belt).

French law requires that you have ID on your person at all times, so you should always carry your passport—in a safe place, and *not* with your money. A lost passport is easier to replace if you have a photocopy of the first few pages of the passport that was lost. The U.S. Embassy handles passports and visas at 2-4, rue Gabriel in the 8th Arr. on the northwest corner of Place de la Concorde. Call before you go to clarify the passport replacement procedure. The Embassy phone number is (0)1.43.12.22.22. The Embassy is open Mon-Fri., 9:00A-6:00P. U.S. citizens to not need visas to enter France.

Tip: Shockingly under-publicized is the fact that your passport needs to be effective for 3 months AFTER YOU RETURN from your Paris trip in order for you to travel to France. (For a 2-week business trip, it's four months; for a 2-month vacation, it's 5 months.)

Tip: Packing two passport-sized pictures will save you considerable time if you want to avail yourself of certain money-saving resources (see page 74) or in case you should require a replacement passport.

Don't forget an extra pair of prescription glasses or contact lenses. Speaking of prescriptions, take copies of prescriptions for eyewear and medications. Check your airline to determine whether each prescription medication must be in its identifying bottle. If you have chronic health problems or a complex health history, consider taking copies of your most important health records, health proxies, etc.

Pack (but not in your carry-on) an all-purpose knife that includes what we hope will become a frequently used corkscrew. Take frequently used items you may not find easily in Paris: artificial sweetener (take loads if you use it), sunscreen, lip balm, etc. Your U.S. driver's license will suffice for renting a car in France.

Tip: This may sound silly, but consider taking a small magnifying glass for reading maps—maybe one with a light for night use, including reading menus in dimly lit restaurants.

If you're planning to visit a number of paid attractions, you may benefit from purchasing a Paris Museum Pass (La Carte Musée) online in advance or after you arrive in Paris. (See page 112 for details.)

When You Arrive

The euro is presently the unit of currency in France and 24 other European countries. See page 30 for details on currency. If your ATM card accesses one of the popular ATM networks (e.g. CIRRUS or PLUS), you don't need to take a large amount of French currency with you—maybe the equivalent of €200 (€300 on weekends).

Tip: Some ATMs don't display letters— only numbers—on the keys; so know your PIN in numerical terms.

Carry at least 20€ in coins in the airport and in the city. At the airport, you may decide to use line-avoiding ticket-dispensing machines (which may require coins or small bills) for certain airport-to-Paris public transportation. Moreover, Parisians have an aversion to making more than minimal change. At banks or places with large "CHANGE" signs, coins (or "monnaie," pronounced "moah-NEH") are available.

Charles de Gaulle Airport ("Shahrl deh GOAHLL Eye-roah-POAR"), handles most international airline traffic. Often called by its old name, Roissy ("Wruh-SEE"), CDG is 14 miles from the center of Paris. Orly Airport ("Oahr-LEE"), used more for travel within Europe, is about nine miles from the city center.

You'll probably have received an embarkation card on the plane. If you have completely filled out this card before reaching the airport, you've taken your first step toward freeing yourself from airport hassle. To clear up two words on the card that confound many people, "debarkation" means departure and "embarkation" means arrival.

Tip: Remember that a "RENSEIGNEMENT" sign means a <u>source</u> of information; but one <u>asks</u> for "directions" (dee-rek see-ONH).

Upon arrival, follow the crowd to customs ("Douane," pronounced "Dwahn"). You'll need a valid, unexpired passport and your completed embarkation card. Once you're through customs, go to "Bagage" ("Bah-GAZH").

Tip: Free luggage carts are lined up nearby. The supply can be limited; so seek out a cart immediately and guard it carefully.

If your luggage does not appear, file a report at the nearby counter, where English will be spoken. The airlines are usually good about delivering lost luggage to the owner's hotel the next day.

With luggage in hand (or on a cart), head for the exit ("Sortie"). You'll see two signs: "Rien à Déclarer" (Nothing to Declare) and "A Declarer" (Something to Declare). If you have nothing to declare upon entering France, head briskly to the "Rien à Declarer" sign and leave. Except in unusual circumstances, your exit should be smooth.

Tip: Hesitation in departing could be misconstrued as indecision about declaring something. Don't run, but don't dawdle.

Tip: For the ten most useful French terms, refer to page 45. More extensive vocabulary begins on page 46, but these ten words should at least get you on your way to the city. (Also refer to pages 67-68 if you'll be taking a taxi.)

Tip: After a long, fatiguing trip, we would sacrifice the cost of a meal in order to enjoy the comfort and directness of a taxi from the airport. But weekday rush hours can make it a long, expensive ride.

Transportation to Paris

Several transportation alternatives from the airport to Paris (and back) exist. We'll cover those we think are most worth considering. For additional options, see: http://www.parisnet.com/info_airplane.html

The main variables in selecting a mode of transportation are:

1. Ease of access at the airport

2. Cost

3. Duration of transport

4. Directness of the transport from the airport to your door

5. Comfort

<u>Taxis</u> (gratuity = 10%-20%)

Access: Taxi line (moves fast) outside at point where you depart customs.

Cost to Central Paris:	40€-70€ from CDG, 25€-50€ from Orly (plus tip). Add €1 per piece of luggage carried in the trunk.
Duration:	30-40 minutes in light traffic, 90-120 minutes at rush hour.
Directness:	Will take you to your door with no side stops.
Comfort:	You have taxi to yourself; driver may smoke (you may request him not to).
Misc.:	Make certain taxi has meter that starts only when you enter. If you speak no French, refer to pages 67-68 to instruct driver.

Paris Airport Shuttle (gratuity: 10%-15%)

http://www.paris-airport-shuttle.com/orly_shuttle.htm

Access:	(CDG pickup): English-speaking driver will pick you up at your terminal. Before getting luggage, use any airport phone booth to dial a toll-free number displayed on your confirmation so they will be ready to pick you up.
Cost:	Either airport: 27€ for 1 person, 19.90€ per person for 2-3 people, 17€ per additional person, child under 10 = 12€
Duration:	45 minutes to 2 hours depending on traffic, passenger load
Directness:	Goes to your door, but shared van; yours may not be first stop.
Comfort:	Non-smoking, air-conditioned.
Misc.:	Make advance reservations: from U.S. 011-33 (1) 79.97.60.04

R.E.R. B Métro Line Serving Charles de Gaulle Airport
(http://europeforvisitors.com/paris/articles/paris-cdg-ground-transportation-trains.htm)

Access: 5:00A-12:00P every 15 minutes
                   R.E.R. Line 1 serves Terminals 1, 3
                   R.E.R. Line 2 serves Terminal 2
                   Either take free airport shuttle train (CDGVAL from
                   any terminal) or walk to R.E.R. from Terminals 2 or 3.

                   Buy an R.E.R. ticket that will allow you to transfer
                   from the train station in Paris to a local Métro train
                   that will get you reasonably close to your hotel. But
                   you'll still likely to have to do at least some
                   walking (potentially including a lot of Métro steps).

Cost: 8.40€ per adult, 5.90€ per child age 4-10

Duration: 30-45 minutes

Directness: This alternative requires a lot of logistical shuffling,
                   which will be exacerbated by the weight of
                   your luggage.

Comfort: You'll probably get a seat during the entire trip to Paris, but the
                   transfers may get old in a hurry.

*Tip: Departing Paris can take much longer than arrival. We'd allow
two to three hours AT THE AIRPORT just to be on the safe side. It
can be amazingly disorganized, with exceptionally long lines and
unexpected challenges. One time, we even found our taxi bogged
down by an impromptu truckers' strike and were extremely lucky to
catch our plane.*

Crash Course in Paris Geography

At first, Paris seems sprawling and complex. Visitors have a choice:

- Give in to feelings of confusion, thereby limiting sightseeing mainly to programmed tours and focusing on the most obvious attractions

- **or** expand their Parisian horizons by learning just the following facts that will reveal Paris to be surprisingly well-organized, with just enough quirks to offer a virtual cornucopia of intriguing options.

As shown on the following outline map, Paris is organized into districts called arrondissements ("ahr-awn deese-MAWNH"), which are numbered in serpentine fashion beginning at the center of the city from #1 (Louvre area) through #20 (eastern outskirts). The various arrondissements reflect a great diversity of neighborhood subcultures. Major features of each arrondissement are listed on pages 118-125.

The River Seine (pronounced "**Senn**,"*not* "Sayne") defines Paris geographically and is the city's spiritual life blood. The river roughly bisects Paris, flowing approximately east to west and separating the northern and southern portions of the city. Two islands—Ile de la Cité and Ile St.- Louis— lie in the middle of the Seine.

Mort Rosenblum, in his great book *The Secret Life of the Seine* (most recently printed in 2001), theorizes that one may discern the state of all France and much of the world by watching the Seine. Are the barges riding low due to the weight of gravel? (This suggests a booming construction industry). Is the river running fast, high and cocoa brown in April? (The skiing season must have been great.) In the past, smiling Soviet barge captains were a harbinger of détente.

If one were (ugh!) floating in the direction of the muddy east-to-west current of the Seine, the northern section of Paris would be on the right; thus it's called the Right Bank—center of commerce, luxury and tourist attractions. The southern section, the Left Bank, is historically more of a population melting pot with an intellectual, literary, activist heritage. You'll see more monuments and chic on the Right Bank and more of authentic, everyday Parisian life on the Left Bank.

The Arrondissements of Paris

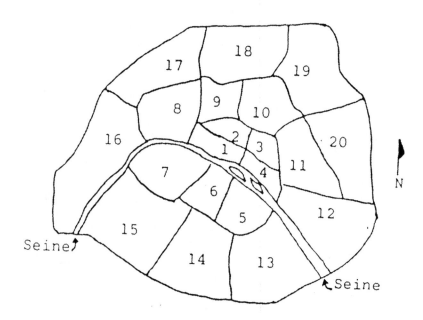

In Paris, five-digit Postal Codes (the equivalent of U.S. Zip Codes) begin with the three digits "750." The last two digits coincide with the number of the arrondissement they represent. For example a Postal Code of 75007 reflects the 7th Arr., and 75014 indicates the 14th Arr.

Tip: Most street signs (often displayed on the facades of street-corner buildings) include arrondissement numbers.

Getting Your Bearings

The Seine is the reference point for street numbers throughout Paris.

• On streets roughly parallel to the Seine, street numbers ascend from east to west (the direction in which the river flows).

• On streets that run in a southerly-northerly direction, street addresses begin at the Seine and ascend as one moves away from the river. If you cross a bridge, you'll find that the street name changes.

• On Ile de la Cité and Ile St.-Louis (in the middle of the Seine), addresses on south-north streets ascend from south to north as on the Right Bank. (Both islands lie within Right Bank arrondissements.)

Another approach to directional orientation is to look for certain prominent landmarks:

• Notre Dame Cathedral (on Ile de la Cité) is the exact city center.

• The Eiffel Tower is in the western part of the city (on the Left Bank), and the huge rectangular arch of La Défense is to the west and outside of the city proper.

• Sacré Coeur's gleaming white domes are to the north (Right Bank).

• No really notable easterly landmark exists, although the Panthéon (with its large copper dome and cupola) is in a generally southeasterly direction (on the Left Bank).

• The 59-story Tour (Tower) Montparnasse is to the south.

A ring of major auto routes ("périphériques") surrounds Paris.

Tip: A complete list of streets, displaying their arrondissements and Métro access, appears in ***Paris par Arrondissement*** *(see page 170).*

21

Selecting Your Neighborhood

From the many diverse districts in Paris, we recommend that you select a hotel in a location consistent with your personality and priorities. We have selected seven neighborhoods that we consider candidates (displayed in no particular order). All offer good hotels:

The Marais (Right Bank—portions of 3rd and 4th Arrondissements)

Right Bank mixture of quiet residences, museums (Carnavalet, Victor Hugo, Picasso), excellent restaurants, "happening" nightlife; the must-see oldest public square in Paris (Place des Vosges); favored by many gays. Interesting mix of trendy fashion boutiques and more traditional shops.

Champs-Etoile (Right Bank—8th Arrondissement)

Right Bank excitement and diversity: Champs Elysées; Arc de Triomphe; landmark restaurants interspersed with American fast food joints; user-friendly for tourists who don't mind being patronized to some extent; pickpocket heaven; service-oriented accommodations—from small hotels on relatively quiet back streets to luxury hotels such as the Four Seasons Hôtel George V (or George Cinq).

Ile St.-Louis (Right Bank—4th Arrondissement)

Island in the Seine; most remarkable attributes are antiquity, wealth, stillness right in the middle of the city, and proximity to the river and a vast number of Paris attractions; a few good restaurants, small hotels, and a world-famous ice cream and sorbet shop (Berthillon).

Latin Quarter (Left Bank—portions of 5th and 6th Arrondissements)

Left Bank melting pot; student quarter (Sorbonne—hence the "Latin" designation); superb people-watching in Place St.-Michel; loads of restaurants—venerable and newer; jazz clubs; Roman ruins (Musée de Cluny); Bohemian Mouffetard area; historic Shakespeare & Company bookstore; near the Seine and Notre Dame.

Odéon-Luxembourg (Left Bank—6th Arrondissement)

Quiet Left Bank area, but on the fringe of the Latin Quarter; literary echoes resound; focal point of the famed "Lost Generation" of American expatriates (Hemingway, etc.) in the twenties and thirties; Luxembourg Garden is fabulous and contains something for everyone; Parisian tradition, from the restaurants to the shops.

Sèvres-Bac (Left Bank—7th Arrondissement)

The southern portion of this Left Bank arrondissement is relatively quiet with a residential orientation, boutiques, quaint parks, a luxury Hôtel (Lutétia), oldest department store (Le Bon Marché), Grand Epicérie (grocery store with mouth-watering food displays—but you'll have to bag your own groceries), Japanese pagoda-style theatre, 15 minutes walk to the Seine and Latin Quarter. The northern part is more lively (restaurants, open markets, especially on Rue Cler and Rue St.-Dominique), Eiffel Tower, Musée d'Orsay).

Montparnasse (Left Bank—13th and 14th Arrondissements)

During the French Revolution, cafés in this Left Bank district were the frenzied core of Parisian Bohemia; during the early 1900s, Montparnasse was a major focus of literature and art; historic cafés (La Coupole, La Dôme, Le Select, La Rotonde) remain. A distance from most Paris attractions—but if you're a fanatic for café life, this could be the spot for you.

Selecting a Hotel

Paris hotels are everywhere. You should first decide whether you are a large-hotel person (emphasis on services and luxury) or a small-hotel person (emphasis on Paris authenticity and value). Should your hotel be a major element of what makes Paris special for you? Or should it be more of a functional, hopefully comfortable place to recharge your personal batteries? Relatively small hotel rooms are the rule rather than the exception, as physical space in Paris is at a premium.

Parisian hotels are rated on a four-star scale by the government. The star system works thusly:

None	√ Very basic; may or may not be very clean; perhaps no maid service
	√ Few, if any, private bathrooms
	√ Staff may speak only French
*	√ Low prices don't always represent true value on a sight-unseen basis
	√ No frills; usually clean; small and intimate; maid service
	√ Front desk staff usually understands at least some English
	√ Some have elevators (often called "lifts"), direct-dial, tv
	√ Majority of rooms have private bathrooms
	√ May have a breakfast nook, but never a full restaurant
**	√ Many good bargains, particularly due to locations
	√ Nice furnishings (antiques in some, plain in others); small and intimate
	√ Front desk staff usually bilingual, at least to a degree
	√ Usually have elevators ("lifts")
	√ Rooms are comfortable with private bathrooms in most rooms
	√ Direct-dial phones and television in all rooms
	√ More likely to have a dining nook than a full restaurant
	√ Availabiity and types of amenities, e.g. air conditioning, can vary
***	√ A step below the most luxurious hotels (and usually smaller)
	√ Very comfortable; air conditioning probable
	√ Front desk staff will speak English very well
	√ Always have elevator ("lift"), private bath, direct-dial, television
	√ May have a restaurant, probably mini bars in rooms
****	√ Expensive; often less intimate; pay the price to hobnob with affluence
	√ Usually very large, catering to tourists and businesspeople
	√ Ultimate in comfort, service, furnishings
	√ Front desk staff speaks English and may dote on clients
	√ Elevator, private bath, direct-dial, tv, invariably a minibar
	√ Occasionally a swimming pool (George Cinq, Bristol, Vendôme)
	√ Full restaurant—sometimes elite

A **luxury hotel** can charge 300€ or far upward per night. A sampling:

Left Bank:

Hôtel Lutétia (6th Arr.); 45, blvd. Raspail; Interesting facade, WWII history
T: (0)1.49.54.46.46 F: (0)1.49.54.46.00 www.lutetia-paris.com

L'Hôtel (6th Arr.); 13, Rue des Beaux-Arts: Think Oscar Wilde, Jim Morrison
T: (0)1.44.41.99.00 F: (0)1.43.25.64.81 www.hotel.com

Hôtel de l'Abbaye (6th Arr.); 10, rue Cassette: Former abbey, friends raved about it
T: (0)1.45.44.38.11 F: (0)1.45.48.07.86 www.l-hotel-abbaye.com

Right Bank (where most grand hotels are located):

Plaza Athenée (8th Arr.); 25, ave. Montaigne: Very fashionable; superb restaurant
T: (0)1.53.67.66.65 F: (0)1.53.67.66.66 www.plaza-athenee-paris.com

Hôtel de Crillon (8th Arr.); 10, pl de la Concorde: Elite; choice of many dignitaries
T: (0)1.44.71.15.00 F: (0)1.44.71.15.02 www.crillon-paris.com

Four Seasons George V (8th Arr.); 31, av. George V: Plush. Recently renovated
T: (0)1.49.52.70.00 F: (0)1.49.52.70.10 www.fourseasons.com/paris

Below the grand hotel level are many excellent **three-star hotels**, at which a double room can cost 150€+ per night, although some offer occasional bargains that can be substantial. Most conveniences are offered. We have toured each of the following three-star hotels and have found all to be very acceptable.

Left Bank:

Hôtel Claude Bernard Saint Germain: 43, rue des Ecoles (5th Arr.)
Borders Sorbonne and Latin Quarter action; tiny elevator
T: (0)1.43.26.32.52; F: (0)1.43.26.80.56
W: www.hotelclaudebernardparis.com

Hôtel Saint-Germain; 88, rue du Bac (7th Arr.)
Street of shops and antiques, not far from the Seine, Musée d'Orsay
T: (0)1.49.54.70.00; F: (0)1.45.48.26.89
W: www.hotelsaintgermain.com

Hôtel Jardin de l'Odéon; 7, rue Casimir DeLavigne (6th Arr.)
Heart of quiet Odéon; walk to Latin Quarter, Seine, Luxembourg Garden
T: (0)1.53.10.28.50; F: (0)1.43.25.28.12
W: www.hoteljardinodeonparis.com

Hôtel Chomel; 15, rue Chomel (7th Arr.)
Quiet residential Sévres-Bac area; near shopping, conveniences, parks
T: (0)1.45.48.55.52; F: (0)1.45.48.89.76
W: www.chomel.com

Right Bank:

Hôtel des Deux-Iles; 59, rue St.-Louis-en-l'Ile (4th Arr)
On Ile St.-Louis; quiet and yet in the heart of Paris near the Seine
T: (0)1.43.26.13.35; F: (0)1.43.29.60.25
W: www.2iles.com

Hôtel Saint-Paul le Marais; 8, rue de Sévigné (4th Arr.)
In the old, now-trendy Marais; conveniences, restaurants nearby
T: (0)1.48.04.97.27; F: (0)1.48.87.37.04
W: www.hotel-paris-marais.com

Hôtel Caron de Beaumarchais; 12, rue Vielle-du-Temple (4th Arr.)
In the old, now-trendy Marais; conveniences, restaurants nearby
T: (0)1.42.72.34.12; F: (0)1.42.72.34.63
W: www.carondebeaumarchais.com/

Hôtel Monceau Etoile; 64, rue de Lévis (17th Arr.)
Residential area; near the Seine and major attractions; exceptional hosts
T: (0)1.42.27.33.10; F: (0)1.42.27.59.58
W: www.paris-hotel-monceau.com

Paris is teeming with charming, small two-star hotels—much more so, for instance, than in London. A good double room with private bath normally costs 100-150€ per night, but check for special offers. Employees seem to take a proprietary interest in their hotels, so service may be more amiable.

Having made unannounced tours of the following two-star hotels, we feel comfortable in recommending each of them:

Left Bank:

Hôtel Lindbergh; 5, rue Chômel (7th Arr.)
Quiet Sèvres-Bac area; near shopping, conveniences; particularly hospitable
T: (0)1.45.48.35.53; F: (0)1.45.49.31.48
W: www.hotellindbergh.com

Grand Hôtel des Balcons; 3, rue Casimir Delavigne (6th Arr.)
In the heart of quiet Odéon with Blvd. St-Germain nearby
T: (0)1.46.34.78.50; F: (0)1.46.34.06.27
W: www.balcons.com

Right Bank:

Hôtel d'Albion; 15, rue de Penthièvre (8th Arr.)
Near major attractions, Champs Elysées, dept stores, wonderful hosts
T: (0)1.42.65.84.15; F: (0)1.49.24.03.47
W: www.hotelalbion.net

Selecting a good two-star hotel requires some care:

• To expedite phone negotiations, call Monday-Friday, 9:00A- 4:00P Paris time; night workers may not speak much English.

• For a private bath, specify "salle de bain ('bangh') privée." For a shower, add "avec douche" ("doosh"); for a tub, add "avec baignoire ('bangh-wahr')."

• Ask about air conditioning in summer. It may be essential, unless room is very well-ventilated and is not immediately under the roof.

• Ask which credit cards are accepted; some hotels accept no cards.

• Most Paris hotels now have some version of WiFi, but make certain.

• There is no smoking allowed in Paris hotels (and restaurants). Upper hotel floors can distance you from exterior smoke and noise as well as yielding the best views. Avoid courtyard exposures if you have an aversion to smoke or to possible noise from other rooms.

• Ask whether the price ("tarif") includes breakfast ("petit déjeuner"), which will be continental if available. It may be more interesting (though perhaps more expensive) to go out for breakfast, especially if you like to people-watch.

Adaptations and Conversions

You'll feel at home pretty quickly in a large hotel, if only because the staff will insist on it. If you want to feel a little more French and save more of your euros for dining, a smaller hotel is the place. The tradeoff is that you may have to "accommodate the accommodations" in smaller hotels to some degree.

- Most hotels tend to have small rooms, so be prepared to adapt. You may have to place some clothing in piles on closet shelves. Some hotels can be stingy with coat hangers. Consider packing a few.

- If your small hotel provides only one bath towel per room, ask for "une serviette de bain supplémentaire" (pronounced "eywn sehr-vee-EHTT deh BANH soo-pleh-mahng-TEHR").

- Don't be surprised to find no shower curtain. The shower may be a hand-held nozzle that can also be placed on a fixture to approximate an overhead shower. It can take more than one try to get the hang of using this device without spraying the bathroom floor.

- Years ago, guests were expected to furnish their own soap, and you may find only one small piece of facial soap in the bathroom. If you feel strongly about this issue (interpret "strongly" as you wish), take your own soap—but hide it like gold whenever you leave the room.

- Paris tap water is purified and okay to drink, but three-quarters comes from the Seine; so it pays to keep some bottled water in your room. In cool weather, if you have no mini bar, use your outdoor balcony to chill beverages at night. Bottled water, soft drinks, and even some wine and beer may be available at your front desk.

These cautions are intended to be realistic but not off-putting. In fact, we wouldn't stay anywhere but in a small hotel—generally a two-star hotel—in Paris; and we like our creature comforts.

Tip: The later you sleep in the morning and stay out at night, the less you're forcing your body to adapt to the intercontinental time change. (What a rationalization!)

Electricity

Paris operates on an electrical current of 220 volts. You'll need an adapter for U.S. appliances that operate on 110 volts. Adapters are usually available in U.S. electronics or hardware stores. You'll need an adaptor with two rounded prongs on one side and two slots and an oval hole on the other side. In Paris, they're available at the BHV (Bazaar de l'Hôtel de Ville), a bargain department store at 52-64, rue de Rivoli, 4th Arr. Tel. (0)1.42.74.90.00 Métro: Hôtel-de-Ville

If your appliance has a built-in converter, it may include two settings. Check the directions to determine which one converts 220 voltage to 110. A friend used the wrong setting and found her curling iron melting like the Wicked Witch of the North.

Internet

Most hotels now offer WiFi internet access. Check before reserving. Cyber-cafés are popular; pay as you play. French keyboards are different from U.S. boards; ask for a "QWERTY version." A few cyber cafés, with arrondissement and phone numbers, appear below. They're not always the most stable enterprises, so phone before going.

Au Web 46; 46, rue du Roi de de Sicile (4th Arr.); (0)1.40.27.02.89

Paris-Cy Internet Café; 8, rue de Jouy (4th Arr.); (0)1.42.71.37.37

Planet Cyber Café: 173, rue de Vaugirard, (15th Arr.); (0)1.45.67.71.14

Jardin de l'Internet: 79, blvd. St.-Michel (5th Arr.); (0)1.44.07.22.20

Baguenaude Café: 30, rue de la Grande Truanderie (1st Arron.); (0)1.40.26.27.74

Milk Internet Hall; six cafés in Paris; 70-200 computers per location; free Skype

Bastille area: 20, rue du Faubourg Saint-Antoine (12th Arron.): (0)1.43.40.03.00
Les Halles area: 31, boulevard Sébastopol (1st Arron.): (0)1.40.13.06.51
Montparnasse area: 5,rue Odessa (14th Arron.): (0)1.43.20.10.37
Bastille area: 20, rue de Faubourg St.-Antoine (1st Arron.): (0)1.43.40.03.00 (open 24/7)
Opéra area: 28, rue de Quartre-Septembre (2nd Arron.): (0)1.43.40.03.00
Panthéon area: 17, rue Soufflot (5th Arron): (0)1.43.54.55.55 (open 24/7)
Latin Quarter area: 53, rue de la Harpe (5th Arron.): (0)1.44.07.38.89 (open 24/7)

For computer hotspots, see: http://www.wi-fihotspotlist.com/browse/intl/2000010/p1.html

For come-to-you computer repair 24/7, try Ordigood: 06.22.42.84.77.

Currency

On January 1, 2002, the euro ("ew-whro"—symbol €) replaced the franc as the official currency. Consult the following site for current Euro/Dollar conversion rates: http://www.xe.com/ucc/. In France, the term "centime" ("sawnh-TEEM") is preferred over the word "cent" ("sawnh"), which is used in the rest of Europe. The plural, "centimes," is pronounced the same as the singular, with no "s" sound. Be sure to check the exchange rate when you leave for Paris.

Bank notes are worth 5€, 10€, 20€, 50€, 100€, 200€ or 500€. The coins are worth 1, 2, 5, 10, 20 and 50 centimes and 1€ and 2€.

We conducted our own research on rates of currency exchange and concluded that credit cards give the best rate. Allowing for exchange fees and commissions, the rankings were as follows:

1. Credit cards   2. ATMs   3. Banks   4. "CHANGE" establishments

Temperature

European temperatures are expressed in degrees Celsius. To convert Celsius (C) to Fahrenheit (F), multiply the Celsius reading by 1.8; then add 32. To convert Fahrenheit to Celsius, subtract 32; then divide the remainder by 1.8. To save time, consult the following chart:

C	F	C	F	C	F
- 3	27	10	50	23	73
- 2	28	11	52	24	75
- 1	30	12	54	25	77
0	32	13	55	26	79
1	34	14	57	27	81
2	36	15	59	28	82
3	37	16	61	29	84
4	39	17	63	30	86
5	41	18	64	31	88
6	43	19	66	32	90
7	45	20	68	33	91
8	46	21	70	34	93
9	48	22	72	35	95

Normal body temperature of 98.6 degrees Fahrenheit converts to 37 degrees Celsius. (The Celsius system does not utilize decimals.)

Apparel and Shoe Sizes

Following is an aid in converting U.S. sizes to French equivalents:

Women's Coats /	U.S.	8	10	12	14	16	18	
Dresses / Suits	French	36	38	40	42	44	46	
Women's	U.S.	8	8 1/2	9	9 1/2	10	10 1/2	
Stockings	French	35	36	38	39	40	41	
Women's	U.S.	4	5	6	7	9	10	
Shoes	French	35	36	38	40	42	43	
Men's	U.S.	34	36	38	40	42	44	46
Suits / Overcoats	French	44	46	48	50	52	54	56
Men's	U.S.	14	15	15 1/2	16	16 1/2	17	
Shirts	French	36	38	39	40	41	42	
Men's	U.S.	7	7 1/2	8 1/2	9	10	11	12
Shoes	French	39	40	41	42	43	44	45

Time

Paris is six hours ahead of Eastern Time in the U.S. (Paris observes daylight Savings Time when the U.S. does.) When it's noon in Paris, it's 6 a.m. in Boston, 5 a.m. in Chicago, 4 a.m. in Denver, and 3 a.m. in San Francisco.

Lengths

If you're driving in France, the mileage on signs is presented in kilometers. One kilometer equals 5/8 of a mile. A speed of 100 kilometer (km) per hour equals 62.5 miles per hour. Fortunately, the speedometer in your rental vehicle will probably be in kilometers.

One meter equals 3.28 feet or 1.093 yards; 91.5 centimeters = 1 yard
One centimeter equals 0.394 of an inch; 1 inch = 2.54 centimeters

Weights

One kilogram = 2.2 pounds; 909 kilograms = one ton
500 grams = 1.2 pounds; 1 pound = 416.7 grams

Volume

One liter equals 2.1 pints or 1.06 quarts or 33.8 ounces
1 quart =.943 liter; 1 pint = .476 liter; 1 ounce = .03 liter

Synopsis: A Seamless Arrival

- Best months to go (in order): June, May, September. Summer = tourist overload; winter less costly but dark, damp, cold

- Emphasize casual comfort clothes; no shorts; walking shoes preferable to sneakers; sport jacket doesn't hurt at night, but reserve dresses and ties for the most expensive restaurants.

- Take 200€-300€ to keep you afloat until you have access to an ATM. Try to have at least 20€ in French coins or small bills with you at all times.

- Be sure to take an ATM card, plenty of artificial sweetener (if you use it), and extra eyeglasses or contacts.

- In selecting transportation from the airport, consider time of day (especially if it's rush hour) and the tradeoff between expense and the convenience of unshared, door-to-door service and lack of stairs.

- Paris is organized in 20 arrondissements arranged in serpentine fashion, with the Seine as a dividing line. The Right Bank (more luxury, monuments, commerce, tourism, service, detached civility) is to the north of the Seine; and the Left Bank (more informal and genial, greater diversity, literary and academic history) to the south. Ile de la Cité and Ile St. Louis are islands in the middle of the Seine.

- From a wide range of possibilities, select a neighborhood and a hotel with features to suit your personality, lifestyle and pocketbook. The fewer stars the hotel has, the more questions you need to ask before committing. Especially important to consider: availability of elevator ("lift"), air conditioning in summer, Internet access.

- Be prepared to adapt your hotel to your needs, packing resources such as electrical adapters and a couple of extra coat hangers.

- Credit cards and ATMs yield better rates of exchange than banks or currency establishments marked "CHANGE."

Bonding with Paris

Your Personal Sanctuary in Paris

We've mentioned that what most makes Paris special for us is the kinds of people we become while we're there. For each visitor, there is a unique mix of Parisian ingredients that will prove unusually magnetic, will invite repeat visits, and will be indelibly etched in memory. A park, a café, a monument, a park, a children's carousel, a bridge, a walking route—whatever.

Being sensitive to the key components of one's special bond with the city is what we refer to as establishing one's *personal sanctuary in* Paris—a mental "place" to which one may privately retreat in pleasant contemplation whether or not one is in Paris. The next few pages will suggest some steps in shaping one's personal sanctuary.

After settling in, you'll probably be dying to hit the boulevards. A good place to begin is in the neighborhood where you're staying. It will have a "flavor" all its own. Searching for practical neighborhood resources will invariably lead to adventures and discoveries that are the first step in establishing your personal sanctuary. You won't attract glances if you use a securely closed backpack to carry (in combination with your pockets) at least the following resources:

- Your **well-concealed** passport

- Your French currency

- An umbrella

- Bottled water (for a long outing)

- Artificial sweetener (if you use it)

- A pocket knife with a bottle opener (one never knows!)

- A compact book such as *Paris par Arrondissement* (available at many U.S. bookstores and most Paris bookstores), containing a map of Paris, a detailed map of each arrondissement, and an alphabetical listing of all Paris streets with map coordinate references; on long streets, selected street numbers are displayed. (See page 171.)

- A map identifying Métro lines by color (and ideally by number as well)—available free in many places, including most hotel lobbies.

Wherever you walk in Paris, always be on the lookout for future eating places. Menus are posted outside, so you should quickly become practiced in the art of what we call "menu-surfing." (We've even seen people on narrow streets menu-surfing from automobile windows.)

As you explore, note the locations of practical resources such as a mailbox, an ATM, "tabac" shops (they sell stamps and cards necessary for use in most telephone booths—see page 90), a pharmacy, a convenience store, etc. To save time when you have later needs, we suggest that you write addresses as you discover each of the following:

HOTEL _____
METRO STATION_____
TAXI STATION _____
ATM _____
BANK _____
MAIL BOX_____
POST OFFICE_____
TABAC (stamps, phone cards) _____
NEWS KIOSK _____
GROCERY STORE _____
CONVENIENCE STORE_____
DEPT. STORE _____
OUTDOOR MARKET _____
LAUNDRY / CLEANER _____
WINE STORE _____
PHARMACY _____
CHURCH _____
PARK OR GARDEN _____
PARK OR GARDEN _____
THEATRE _____
POLICE STATION_____
CAFE / WINE BAR _____
CAFE / WINE BAR _____
GLACIERE (ice cream store) _____
PATISSERIE (PASTRIES)_____
BREAKFAST PLACE _____
LUNCHEON PLACE _____
LUNCHEON PLACE _____
DINNER PLACE _____
DINNER PLACE _____
DINNER PLACE _____
OTHER _____
OTHER _____

Tip: Afternoon is an ideal time to explore your neighborhood. If you tire or the weather deteriorates, you're close to home base and perhaps a nap, some phone calls, e-mails to the U.S. (which is several hours behind you), or post-card writing. We suggest you do your more demanding and geographically far-reaching exploration in morning and midday hours—when you're freshest.

The more relaxed you are, the more potent your powers of observation. If you're running to a monument, your observational powers are limited. One key to developing your personal sanctuary is to select relaxing vantage points. You may identify several—in or out of your neighborhood. Cafés and parks work best for us.

Tip: Find a pleasant place that offers breakfast items you enjoy at a fair price, and eat every breakfast at the same place every day.

Breakfasts are fairly similar everywhere, so you won't be missing much by sticking with one location. By the third day, especially if your order is similar each day (and if your smile is engaging), odds are the waitperson will recognize you. Voilà! You're now a member of the community. Sure it's short-term; but your spirits have to soar when your day begins with a friendly greeting of recognition thousands of miles from home. What could be more relaxing?

Tip: Weather permitting, try to sit outdoors for breakfast.

An underrated function of breakfast is people-watching. Request an outside location—"dehors" ("deh-OARH") or à l'extérieur ("ah leks-tay ree-EURH"). Watch the uniformed children heading for school and adults going to work. Why are the kids so well-behaved? (Hint: It's related to discipline at home and school.) Why do women, regardless of whether they're dressed elegantly or informally, manage to look so chic? (Their artful use of accessory scarves is a factor.)

You'll begin to notice patterns in the mannerisms and attitudes of the locals. Of course, this is only one neighborhood; things could be different elsewhere.

Tip: Think of a café as a combination oasis and observation post.

For the price of a cup of coffee or a cold drink, you can enjoy a respite from fatigue while ogling the fascinating pedestrian parade from which you just escaped. At most cafés, you can nurse a drink indefinitely without being hassled by the wait staff. The waiter may appear brusque or hurried, but don't interpret this as encouragement to leave. It's more likely an affected mannerism symptomatic of the seriousness with which he takes his job.

Tip: Coca Cola (both regular and diet), fresh orange juice, and fresh lemonade are available at most cafés.

For regular Coca Cola, order "Coca" ("Coah-CAH"). For diet Coca Cola, order "Coca Light." For fresh orange juice or lemonade, order "Orange Pressé" ("Oah-WRAHNZH Pwress-AY") or "Citron Pressé" (See-TWROANH Pwress-AY") respectively. You'll receive a glass of fruit pulp and a separate carafe of water, and you mix the two to taste. Sugar will be provided, but you're on your own for low-calorie sweetener. Pressés are somewhat expensive, and the tartness of the lemon makes a "Citron Pressé" a better bargain because you'll add a lot more water. Bottled apricot and pear juices ("jus d'abricot" and "jus de poire" respectively) are also delicious non-alcoholic drinks.

Tip: To immerse yourself in a pastoral family atmosphere, try a park.

Look for parks that are small and alluring enough to attract a local clientele yet large enough to accommodate a variety of simultaneous activities. Spending an extended period in a park can provide relief from the rigors of walking. You can combine a sampling of nature in an urban environment; an opportunity to observe Parisians of all ages when they're at ease; and maybe (in the right weather) even a sun tan.

We like to settle on a bench in a park that's in a primarily residential area and read while we watch the afternoon age progression. First come the nannies and a few mothers, resuming yesterday's banter while primping their infant charges. Later, the younger school children arrive—sometimes alone but often accompanied by mothers or nannies. They take over the place but are subsequently relegated to perimeter status by older children, who may begin an impromptu soccer game.

A palpable change accompanies the arrival of dads later in the afternoon. Things become more ordered. Nannies begin to disappear. Mothers still converse, and children continue their play. A few dads may even join the soccer game. The tempo and authority have now shifted to the dads; and the corners of all eyes are on them. Their advent has clearly signaled the beginning of the end. Not because people aren't having a good time; but because the indulgence of the benevolent patriarchs is waning.

A park may sound a little dull when one is paying big bucks to be in Paris. Maybe one visit to a local park is more than enough for many. That's what we initially thought. But then we realized how peaceful yet re-energized we felt afterward; how much better we understood Paris having ventured into a grassy haven. Now it's one of our most eagerly anticipated experiences as we wing toward Paris—arguably the ultimate element of our own personal sanctuary.

Tip: Play the detective.

We have found that a key ingredient in identifying one's personal sanctuary involves sharpening one's powers of observation. At home, we spend considerable time on output—trying to influence others in one way or another. In Paris, it's time for intake—watching, listening, digesting and, most especially, imagining.

Notice the inconsequential. Play the detective. Sneak a peek through that courtyard door. You may be rewarded by a gorgeous garden; or perhaps you'll deduce something about the way Parisians live.

Try to fathom the story behind the neatly dressed elderly couple supporting each other as they weave their way through the crosswalk.

You can learn a lot about Parisian life (or perhaps your own) by observing Parisians going about daily life. Efficiently navigating sidewalks (they tend to hug buildings). Shopping in stores (efficiency personified). Walking the children to school (no nonsense, and the well-behaved, backpacked kids seem very happy). Driving their cars (quite aggressive but in control and amazingly accident-free). Striding to or from work (free fashion show). Singing a stirring song during a strike parade (almost a caricature of people taking themselves far too seriously). Taking a casual stroll (female friends tend to walk arm-in-arm). Riding the Métro (a unique culture of its own).

Your Extended Personal Sanctuary

Your neighborhood should not geographically limit your sense of personal sanctuary. Many aspects of Paris that are not near our hotel have nonetheless become part of our *extended* personal sanctuary. A bookstore, a brasserie, an intimate park, a windmill, sunset from a bridge above the Seine—they've all become "old friends." We cherish them, visit them frequently when we're in Paris, and think about them warmly when we're not. The concept of personal sanctuary is really a state of mind—not just a geographic or physical phenomenon.

In your travels around Paris, you'll undoubtedly encounter your own special places and activities away from your neighborhood. You'll enjoy revisiting them; and they'll stick in your mind long after you've left Paris. When you think of them, your immediate world may become temporarily misty. You'll recommend them to others and eagerly await reports. Whether consciously or not, you've added to your extended personal sanctuary.

Being Sensitive and Open to Opportunities

Paris rewards vigilance. Spying a truck delivering the sorbet we'd come to love at a local café, Sally copied an address from the truck. We located the company's store (glaciére) nearby. Triple the flavors!

After her mother passed away, Sally searched everywhere for the right headstone inscription—the Bible, Shakespeare, quotation books, you name it. Nothing seemed perfectly suited to the spirit of this remarkable woman until, while riding in a Paris taxi through Place de la Concorde, Sally spied a quote from the French philosopher, André Malraux, on a bus advertisement: The adage translates to: "Ideas are not just for thinking but for living." This very apropos inscription now memorializes Sally's mother in perpetuity because Sally happened to spot it on a Paris bus.

Paris rewards an outgoing spirit. The primary motivation for one of our Paris trips was to attend a much-heralded Renoir exhibition at the Grand Palais. Included in our luggage was a very large and extremely heavy book called, *Renoir, His Life, His Art, His Letters.* The book is a comprehensive labor of many years of love by a researcher named Barbara Ehrlich White. We felt this tome's enormous reference potential was worth the risk of a luggage-induced hernia.

One evening, while trying a little restaurant near our hotel, we began exchanging Paris observations with the American couple at the next table. At our mention of Renoir, the woman said, "I wrote a book about Renoir." It was unmistakably Barbara Ehrlich White! Dick dashed back to the hotel and lugged the book to the restaurant, where it was autographed and became a focal point among other diners (much to the consternation of waiters). The four of us then went out to a jazz club and got together several times after returning to the U.S. Personal experiences can be important ingredients of one's personal sanctuary.

Paris rewards opportunism. On a Sunday Parisian evening, we asked the couple at the next table how they were enjoying a dish we were considering. One thing led to another, and we learned that they were from New York City. We mentioned that we would soon be visiting Manhattan to see "The Lion King" with daughters and their families. They exclaimed, "Our son is the stage manager of 'The Lion King.'" A few weeks later, our brood was treated to a lengthy, private, backstage tour (including all the puppetry, elevators, and set-changing devices) prior to taking our seats for a wonderful performance. That restaurant has become an important part of our personal sanctuary.

What is it about Paris that impels us to indulge in cross-table conversation—more so than we do it elsewhere? Possibly it's as simple as the fact that Paris is a place for convivial sharing. Maybe an implicit camaraderie is formed by hearing the English language within a French milieu. Perhaps it's the closeness of the tables. It could be the wine. Whatever the stimuli, Parisian restaurant chitchat continues to lead us to revelations and escapades we'll never forget.

Paris rewards endurance. In July, 1989, during the Bicentennial celebration of the French Revolution, the highlight was to be a massive parade down the Champs Elysées. With security barricades all over the place and the Métro teeming, we'd frequently had to walk miles out of our way for several days. In fact, the entire experience convinced us that one national holiday in Paris would suffice for a very long time.

As parade day drew near, we could envision ourselves being herded thirty-deep, as we abortively tried to catch sight of the festivities. We somehow heard (maybe from a desk clerk or more likely through cross-table chatter) about a planned dress rehearsal for the parade at 1:00 in the morning, two days before the actual event. There was no public announcement of the rehearsal. When it comes to public events, Parisian officials seem to be masters of secrecy.

At 1:00 a.m. in Paris, we'd normally be thinking about turning in for the night. In this case, we had decided to take naps earlier in the evening, and we were awakened by our alarm shortly before midnight. "Do we really want to do this?" we drowsily murmured to one another. We dutifully hauled ourselves out of bed and lurched to the Métro, arriving at the Champs Elysées just before 1:00.

Although there were many people on hand, we found openings in the first row behind the restraining ropes. The long parade was absolutely wonderful. When the last float had passed, we turned to head home. The Métro was now closed, and taxis had been quickly gobbled up; so we set out to walk the roughly three barrier-littered miles to our hotel.

We were just crossing a bridge over the Seine, still very near the parade site, when we heard music. Loudspeakers had been strategically placed in trees throughout the entire area, and the musical strains were literally floating from above. It turned out to be the somewhat delayed finale of the parade.

We looked back. Spot-lit on an elevated platform surrounding the obelisk in Place de la Concorde, robed in billowing red, white and blue, was opera diva Jesseye Norman singing the French National Anthem. We consider *The Marseillaise* the most melodically beautiful of the national anthems; but we've always felt that the traditional tempo is a little too fast to allow the melody to take full effect. Well, Ms. Norman was milking every note. She slowly sang the refrain several times, and the chilling phrase, "Aux armes Citoyens," must have consumed at least five to seven seconds each time.

Here we were, free spirits in the middle of our beloved Paris, with this magnificent homage to French history cascading around us as if from the heavens. We stood, transfixed, as the magic enveloped us. Then it ended; and, with tears in our eyes, we turned and walked home in complete silence. Because there was absolutely nothing to say.

You can view Ms. Norman's performance at the parade:
http://www.youtube.com/watch?v=1QQ2k3UpHwQ

Paris rewards persistence. Sometimes you just have to be lucky—but the more one perseveres, the luckier one becomes. Fortified by our experience at the 40th anniversary of D-Day on Omaha Beach (see pages 166-167), we returned two months later for the 40th anniversary of the Liberation of Paris on August 25, 1984. Our expectations were high, considering that we had no idea what to expect.

At home, arrangements would have been emblazoned on the front pages of newspapers—replete with event schedules, etc. Not so in Paris. If the information was in Paris papers, it was well-concealed. We expected a huge parade along the Champs Elysées but were informed by the Office de Tourisme de Paris that any parade would probably be nearer the center of the city. Of course, they had no clue as to an exact location.

So, on August 25th, we set out on foot to canvass central Paris. We saw throngs of tourists and dark blue vehicles transporting police from here to there and back here again—but nothing that consistently suggested the probable location of a parade. We asked several police officers where the parade would be held. To a man, they pursed their lips and feigned no knowledge of any parade—not even in the face of Sally's fluent (and increasingly exasperated) French queries.

We walked and walked in a baking sun, over upwards of six square miles. Our usual refreshment oases—cafés—were overflowing. We had bottled water but didn't want to drink much, because toilets were out of the question. Police pedestrian barriers emerged from nowhere—with no rhyme or reason and unrelated to any apparent parade route.

Finally, after several hours of pure trudgery, we looked at each other and said, "The heck with it" (or somewhat stronger yet fewer words to that effect). Feeling miserable and defeated, we set out on the haphazard, crowd-controlled safari that we hoped would eventually lead to our hotel.

Suddenly, Sally stopped short and said, "What's that sound?" Dick had seen enough war movies to know exactly what it was. Tanks!

We raced toward the thunder. The debilitation of the day quickly dissipated as we spotted tanks rumbling through the streets of Paris—heralding a long parade. Backed up against a bank building by the crowd on the deep Paris sidewalk, we spied windows with gratings above our heads. Somehow we clambered up to the window ledges, hung onto the gratings, and now have home movies of the entire event. Just as our persistence had expired, we had gotten lucky.

****

Over time, we hope you will be moved to treasure elements of your expanding personal sanctuary and experience them even more thoroughly—bringing you closer to them while continually exposing you to additional Parisian insights and discoveries. Congratulations. You're officially bonding with Paris.

Taking Control

In the process of tackling Paris, it's important to exercise as much control as possible over your actions. Otherwise, you'll encounter that old adversary, "Paris by Default"— accepting whatever gratification your environment chooses to mete out to you.

Seizing control requires you to be sufficiently proactive; and, for this, you need to observe the salesman's adage in Meredith Wilson's *"The Music Man." You have to know the territory.* For example:

- We've already discussed the geographic features of Paris (starting on page 19); and they're easily grasped.

- It helps to attempt to speak at least a little French. The French do appreciate the effort even if the execution is flawed. If you don't feel comfortable in this area, we'll give you some help, ranging from bare essentials to more extensive language aids (pages 45-68).

- A working knowledge of transportation alternatives is a must. Aside from walking, you're most likely to use the Métro and taxis, so we'll concentrate on those conveyances while mentioning others.

- Being able to communicate by telephone in Paris has evolved from practically impossible to quite easy. However, you need to know what the options are; and we'll present them.

- A fear of crime can compromise the fun in any big city. In Paris, crimes against tourists are limited mainly to petty theft. We'll acquaint you with several pickpocket schemes so you can delight in thwarting them if the opportunity arises—although we don't expect you to become so confident that you'll be walking down dark alleys with euros sticking out your ears.

- The Paris-related question we get asked most goes something like this: "But what about all those Parisians?" Alleviating concerns about the reputed haughtiness of Parisians involves understanding them better; and we'll help you do just that.

- Ultimately, the upcoming portions of the book should give you a pretty good idea of whether Paris is right for you—and vice versa.

Acquiring Instant French Language Skills

Many Paris tourists worry about their lack of expertise with the French language. But here's an important fact. Parisians appreciate the visitor who makes at least a stab at the beautiful language in which Parisians take justifiable pride. In a sense, refusal to give it a try can be viewed as a slight, especially since most Parisians have gone to the trouble of learning at least some English. This section of the book will provide language assistance for those who need it.

Phonetic pronunciations for many French words appear throughout the book. In multi-syllable words, emphasize the capitalized syllable (almost always the final syllable). The phonetic combination "ay" should be pronounced as in the English word "play." Pronounce "eh" as in the English word "get." The phonetic combination of letters "ew" indicate the sound achieved by trying to say "e" (as in the English word "me") while pursing your lips as if to whistle.

We believe you need only 40 "French Survival" words and phrases to sustain yourself fairly well in Paris—especially if you supplement them with the right body language, gestures, etc. Even if you've never studied French, odds are you already know at least half of the terms.

The Top Ten French Survival Terms

Based on trips not only to France but also to countries where we had no knowledge of the languages, our selections as the ten most essential travel terms are listed below. We'd be absolutely astounded if you don't know at least six of the ten already.

Hello	Bonjour	"Boanh-ZHOOR"
Good-bye	Au revoir	"Oahr-VWA"
Please	S'il vous plaît	"See voo PLEH"
Thank you	Merci	"Mehr-SEE"
You're welcome	De rien	"Derh ree-ANH"
Yes	Oui	"Wee"
No	Non	"Noanh"
How much?	Combien?	"Koahm-BYENH?"
There it is	Voila	"Vwa-LAH"
Do you speak English?	Parlez-vous Anglais?	"Pahr-leh-VOO Awhn-GLAY"

The Remaining 30 French Survival Terms

You'll recognize quite a few of the other 30 French survival terms:

Personal and Conversational

Me	Moi ("Mwah")
You	Vous ("Voo")
Pardon me	Pardonnez-moi (Pahr-doahn-eh-MWAH) (often abbreviated to "Pardon" ("Parh-DOAHNGH") OR Excusez-moi (Ex-kyewz-eh-MWAH) (often abbreviated to "Excusez" ("Ex-kyewz-EH")
I agree	D'accord ("Dah-KOAR")
More slowly	Plus lentement ("Plyew lawnt-MAWNH")

Needs

Police	Police ("Poh-LEESS")
Assistance	Assistance ("Ah-sees-TAHNGHSS")
Hospital	Hôpital ("Owe-pee-TAHL")
Information	Information ("Angh-for-mah-see-ONGH")
Toilet	Toilette ("Twah-LETT")

Getting Around and Communications

Street	Rue ("Wroo")
Métro	Métro ("Meh-TRWOAH")
Taxi	Taxi ("Tahk-SEE")
Telephone	Téléphone ("Teh-leh-FUN")

46

French Survival Terms(Continued)

Accommodations and Dining

Hotel	Hôtel ("Oah-TEHL")
Breakfast	Petit déjeuner ("P'tee deh-zher-AY")
Lunch	Déjeuner ("Deh-zher-NAY")
Dinner	Diner ("Dee-NAY")
Some water	De l'eau ("D'loah")
Some wine	Du vin ("Dyew VANH")
The bill	L'addition ("Ah-dees-YOANH")

Shopping

Store	Magasin ("Mah-gah-ZANH")
Cashier	Caisse ("Kehss")
Floor	Etage ("Eh-TAHZH")

Basement:	Sous-sol	("Soo soahl")(Abbrev. "SS")
Street floor:	Rez de chausée	("Reh deuh shoah-SAY")
2nd floor:	1er étage	("Pruhm-YEHR eh-TAHZH")
3rd floor:	2ème étage	("Dehz-YEHM eh-TAHZH")
4th floor:	3ème étage	("Twahz-YEHM eh-TAHZH")
5th floor:	4ème étage	("Kah-trwee-YEHM eh-TAHZH")

Timing

Morning	Matin ("Mah-TANH")
Afternoon	Après-midi ("Ah-PREH-mee-DEE")
Evening	Soir ("Swahr")
Today	Aujourd'hui ("Oah-zhoor-DWEE")
Yesterday	Hier ("Ee-EHR")
Tomorrow	Demain ("Deh-MANH")

47

Parts of Speech

Some very commonly used pronouns, articles, conjunctions and adjectives:

I	Je "(Zhuh.")
You (familiar form singular)	Tu ("Tyew")
He	Il ("Eel")
She	Elle ("Ell")
We	Nous ("Noo")
You (less familiar or plural)	Vous ("Voo")
They (masc. or both sexes)	Ils ("Eel")
They (fem.)	Elles ("Ell")
The	Le ("Luh.")
A/An (masc.)	Un ("Anh")
A/an (fem.)	Une ("Ewn")
This (masc.)	Ce ("Seuh")
This (fem.)	Cette ("Set")
These (masc. / both sexes)	Ces ("Seh")
These (fem.)	Cettes ("Set")
Some/of (fem.) singular	De ("Deuh")
Some/of (masc.) singular	Du ("Dyew")
Some (plural)	Des ("Deh")
And	Et ("Eh")
But	Mais ("Meh")
For	Pour ("Poor")

Some Handy, Versatile Terms

Five versatile terms can serve you well in a wide variety of situations:

Ça va (Sah-VAH)

> That'll do; This is fine; Works for me; It's okay
> Also, Ça va means "How are you?" (with questioning inflection) or "I'm well."

Je voudrais (Zheuh voo-DREH)...

> I'd like... (followed by either an infinitive or an object)

Où se trouve (Oo-sUh-TRWOOV)...

> Where can one find...? (followed by whatever you seek)
> (Much more cool than "Où est?")

Encore (Awngh-COAR)

> Again; another (for example, a drink refill); more; still
> *Pas* encore (Pahz awngh-CORE) means "Not yet"

Combien (Coahm-bee-YENGH)

> How much? How much does it cost? How many?

The French Alphabet with Phonetic Pronunciations

It may help you to communicate difficult words by spelling them:

A   "Ah"

B   "Beh" (as in "get")

C   "Seh"

D   "Deh"

E   "Euh" (Sounds like the "e" sound in "her," but with open-mouthed "h" at end)

F   "Eff"

G   "Zheh"

H   "Ahsh"

I   "Ee"

J   "Zhee"

K   "Keh"

L   "Ell"

M   "Emm"

N   "Enn"

O   "Owe"

P   "Peh"

Q   "Kyue"

R   "Ehr"

S   "Ess"

T   "Teh"

U   "Ee-YOO "

V   "Veh"

W   "Doobleh-VEH"

X   "Eeks"

Y   "Ee-GREHK"

Z   "Zed"

More Extensive French Language Aids

The 40 survival terms are what you need to *remember* in order to win friends and maybe even influence a few people. An alphabetized list of additionally helpful English-to-French terms begins on page 52. Beside each term, a phonetic pronunciation is shown in parentheses. These pronunciations are not guaranteed to be perfect, but—along with a smile and appropriate gestures—they'll make you understood. Some of the phonetic letter combinations may seem weird; but, if you try your best to articulate them, you'll come close enough.

Three important general guidelines:

* Almost all multi-syllable French words emphasize the last syllable. "Merci" is pronounced "mehr-SEE," *not* "MEHR-see." CAPITAL LETTERS indicate syllables that should be accentuated.

* Most French consonants that appear at the end of words are silent (so "tout" and "tous" are both pronounced "too"). Four ending consonants are **usually** (not always) pronounced, and they're all contained in the English word: **careful**"

    > C   "porc" means pork and is pronounced "pork"
    > R   "or" (the word for gold) is pronounced "oahr"
    > F   "neuf " (the word for nine) is pronounced "neuhf"
    > L   "loyal" means loyal and is pronounced "lwah-YAHL"

* Many declarative French sentences may be turned into questions by elevating your tone at the end of the sentences. "Il fait beau!" indicates it's a nice day. "Il fait beau?" ASKS whether it's a nice day. "Ça va!" means "I'm well." "Ça va?" means, "Are you well?"

Tip: Keep it simple! If you're just learning French, don't try to master various verb tenses. Stick with the present tense, and focus on getting the nouns correct. The right noun, along with proper voice inflection, pointing and a head nod or hand gesture here and there, can go a long way. If you really get stuck, you can always resort to pointing to the equivalent French term in your dictionary or spelling it.

Selected English-to-French Vocabulary Terms

A

A	Un ("Anh") feminine; Une ("Eywn") masculine
Across from	En face de ("Awnh FAHSS duh")
(The) address	(L')adresse ("Lah-DRESS")
After	Après ("Ah-PREH")
Afternoon	Après-midi ("Ah-preh-mee-DEE")
(The) airplane	(L')avion ("Lah-vee-OANH")
(The) airport	(L'aéroport ("La-ay-ro-POAHRR")
An ankle	Une cheville ("Eywn sheh-VEE")
Appetizer	Entrée ("Ahnh-TRAY")
(An) attorney	(Un) avocat ("Anh ah-voah-KAH")
(The) auto	(La) voiture ("Lah vwa-TYEUR")

B

Basement	Sous-sol ("Soo-SOAHL")
(Some) beer	De la bière ("Deuh lah bee-EHR")
Before (time)...	Avant de... ("Ah-VAWNH duh")
(A) bicycle	(Une) bicyclette ("Eywn bee-see-KLETT")
The bill (meal)	L'addition ("Lah-dee-see-OANH")
(The) boat (ship)	(Le) bateau ("Leuh bah-TOAH")
(A) book	(Un) livre ("Anh leev-r")
A bottle	Une bouteille ("Eywn boo-TAY")
Boulevard	Boulevard ("Bool-VARH")
Breakfast	Petit déjeuner ("P'TEE day-zhuh-NAY")
(A) bridge	(Un) pont ("Anh poanh")
(I'm) browsing	Je ne fais que regarder ("Zheh nuh fay kuh reh-gahr-DAY")
(A) building	(Un) bâtiment ("Anh bah-tee-MAWNH")
(The) bus	(L')autobus ("Loah-toah-BOOSS")
To buy	Acheter ("Ahsh-TAY")

C

To cancel a reservation	Annuler de réservation ("Ah-new-LAY duh ray-sehr-vah-see-OANH")
(The) cashier/ checkout	(La) caisse ("Lah kehss")
(The) century	(Le) siècle ("Leuh see-EKL")
(A) coat	(Un) manteau ("Anh mahnh-TOAH")
(It's) cloudy	(Il y a) des nuages ("Eel yah deh nyew-AHZH")
(It's) cold	(Il fait) froid ("Eel feh frwah")
(A) concert	(Un) concert ("Anh koanh-SEHR")
To confirm a	Confirmer une réservation ("Koahn-feer-MAY eywn ray-sehr-reservation vah-see-OANH")
Connection (Métro transfer point)	Correspondence ("Koah-reh-spoanh-DAWNHSS")
A cup	Une tasse ("Eywn tahss")

D

(We've) decided	(Nous avons) décidé ("Noo zahvoangh day-see-DEH")
(It was) delicious	(C'était) délicieux ("Say-teh day-lee-see-EUH")
(A) dentist	(Un) dentiste ("Anh dawnh-TEEST")
Dinner	Dîner ("Dee-NAY")
(Paris) district	Arrondissement ("Ah-roanh-dees-MAWNH")
(A) doctor	(Un) médicin ("Anh mayd-SANH")

E

(The) elevator	(L')ascenseur ("Lah-sawnh-SEUH")
English	Anglais ("Awhn-GLAY")
(That's) enough (That will do)	Ça suffit ("Sah soo-FEE")
Entrance	Entrée ("Ahnh-TRAY")
Escalator	Escalier mécanique ("L'ess-kahl-YEH meh-kahn-EEK")
Evening	Soir ("Swahr")
(I'd like to) exchange __	Je voudrais échanger __ ("Zheh voo-dray eh-shawn-ZHAY") __ n
Excuse me	Excusez-moi ("Excusez-moi (Ex-kyew-zay-MWAH) (often abbreviated to "Excusez" ("Ex-kyew-ZAY")
Exit	Sortie ("Soahr-TEE")
(Too) expensive	(Trop cher ("Trwoah SHEHR")

F

A fork	Une fourchette ("Eywn foor-SHETT")
Fill it (with gas)	Le plein (de petrol) ("Leuh plehn") ("deh pay-TROAL")
Some film (for camera)	Du film ("Dyew feelm")
(We're) finished (meal)	(Nous sommes) terminés ("Noo sum") "tehr-mee-NAY"
The Fire Dept.	Les pompiers ("Lay poahm-pee-AY")
(The) flight	(Le) vol ("Leuh voahl")
Floor (in store)	See "Level"
Forbidden	Interdit ("Anh-tehr-DEE")
French	Français ("Frahnh-SEH")
From	De "(Deh") (D' if next word starts with a vowel)
(In) front of	Devant ("Deh-VAWNH")
(I'm) full (food)	(Je suis) satisfait ('Zheh swee") "sah-tees-FEH"

G

Go	Allez ("Ahl-LAY")
Good-bye	Au revoir ("Oahr-VWA")
Good day (Hello)	Bonjour ("Boanh-ZHOOR")
Good evening	Bonsoir ("Boanh-SWAHR")
Good night	Bonne nuit ("Bun HWEE")
(A) glass	Un verre ("Eywn vehrr")

H

A handbag (pocketbook)	Un sac à main ("Anh sahk ah MAGNH")
(Don't) hang up (Hold the line)	(Ne) quittez (pas) ("Neh") "kee-TAY" ("pah")
A hat	Un chapeau ("Anh shah-POAH")
He	Il ("Eel")
Hello / Good day	Bonjour ("Boahn-ZHOOR")
Help (aid)	Assistance ("Ah-sees-TAHNSS")
Help (trouble)	Au secours! ("Oah seh-COOR")
Here (location)	Ici ("Ee-SEE")
Here it is	Voici ("Vwah-SEE")
(A) hospital	(Un) hôpital ("Oah-pee-TAHLL")
The American Hospital	L'Hôpital Américain ("Loah-pee-TAHLL Ah-meh-ree-KANH")
(It's) hot	(Il fait) chaud ("Eel feh shoah")
Hotel	Hôtel ("Owe-TELL")
(The) house	(La) maison ("Lah meh-ZOANH")
How are you?	Ça va bien? ("Sah vah BYANH?") (or just "Ça va?")
How do you do?	Comment allez-vous? ("Koah-mawn-tah-leh VOO?")
How does one say...	Comment dire ... ("Koah-moanh DEER" ...)
How much/ how many?	Combien? ("Kohm-BYENH")

I

I	Je ("Zheh")
(Some) ice	Des glaçons ("Deh ("glah-SONH")
(I'm) ill	(Je suis) malade ("Zheh swee mah-LAHD")
In	Dans ("Dawnh")
Information (facts)	Information ("Anh-foar-mah-see-OANH")
Information (source)	Renseignements ("Rawnh-sehn-yuh-MAHNH")

K

A knife	Un couteau ("Anh coo-TOAH")
Kilometer (0.6 of a mile)	Kilometre ("Kee-loah-MEHTR")
(I don't) know (no knowledge)	(Je ne) sais (pas) ("Zhehn") "seh" ("pah")

L

Last (final/ previous	Dernier ("Dehrn-YAY")
(Until) later	(A) bientôt ("Ah byanh-TOAH")
(To the) left	(A) gauche ("Ah goash")
Level (store)	Etage ("Eh-TAHZH")

Basement: Sous-sol ("Soo sohl")(Abbreviation "SS")
Street floor: Rez de chausée ("Reh deuh show-SAY")
2nd floor: 1er étage ("Pruhm-YEH eh-TAHZH")
3rd floor: 2ème étage ("Dehz-YEHM eh-TAHZH")
4th floor: 3ème étage ("Twahz-YEHM eh-TAHZH")
5th floor: 4ème étage ("Kah-trwee-YEHM eh-TAHZH")

(I'd) like ...	(Je) voudrais ... ("Zheh") ("voo-DREH" ...)
(I'm) looking for...	Je cherche.. ("Zheh shehrsh")
(I've) lost...	(J'ai) perdu... ("Zheh pehr-DYEW")
Lunch	Déjeuner ("Day-zheuh-NAY")

56

M

(A) magazine	(Une) revue ("Eywn") ("reh-VYEW")
(The) main course	Le plat principal ("Leuh") ("plah prwangh-see-PAHL")
(A) map	(Une) carte ("Eywn") (kart")
Me	Moi ("Mwah")
Medium (steak)	A point ("Ah pwangh")
The menu	La carte ("Lah kahrt")
(Some) milk	(Du) lait ("Dew") ("leh")
Miss	Mademoiselle ("Mahd-mwah-ZEHLL")
(This) month	(Ce) mois ("Seuh") ("mwah")
Morning	Matin ("Mah-TANH")
(A) movie	(Un) spectacle ("Anh") ("spek-TAHKL")
Mrs. or adult female	Madame ("Mah-DAHM")
(I) must...	(Je) dois... (Zheh") ("drwah"...)

N

(In the) name of	(Au) nom de ("Oah") "noam" ("deuh")
(My) name is ___	Je m'appel ___ ("Zheh mah-PELL ___ ")
(Bldg.) number	Numéro ("Neuh-may-ROAH")
(Phone) number	Numéros de téléphone ("Neu-meh-ROAH deh tay-lay-FUN")
(Your) name	(Votre) nom ("Votr") ("noamh")
A napkin	Une serviette ("Eywn sehr-vee-ETT")
Near	Près ("Preh")
The necktie	La cravate ("Lah krah-VAHTT")
Neighborhood	Quartier ("Kahr-tee-AY")
(A) newspaper	(Un) journal ("Anh") ("zhoor-NAHL")
Next	Prochain ("Proah-SHENH")
Night	Nuit ("Nweeh")
No	Non ("Noanh")
No one	Personne ("Pehr-SUN")
Non-smoking section	L'espace non-fumeur ("Less-PAHSS noanh-few-MEUHR")

57

O

(An) office	(Un) bureau ("Anh") ("byeuw-RWOAH")
Okay (I agree)	D'accord ("Dah-KOARH")
On	Sur ("Syeur")
(May we eat) outdoors?	(Nous pouvons dîner) dehors? ("Noo poo-VOANGH dee-NAY") "deh-OARH?")
Over	Au dessus de ("Oh deh-SYEU deh")
Overcooked	Trop cuit ("Trwoah KWEE")

P

Pajamas	Le pyjama ("Leuh pee-jah-MAH")
The pants (outer)	Les pantalons ("Leh pahn-tah-LOANGH")
Pantyhose	Un collant ("Anh koahll-AWNH")
Pardon me	Pardonnez-moi ("Pahr-DOAH-neh-MWAH") (often abbreviated to "Pardon" ("Parh-DOAHNGH")
(The) parking	(Le) parking ("Leuh pahr-KEENH")
(A) party	(Une) fête ("Eywn") ("feht")
(A birthday) party	Une fête de la naissance ("Eywn feht deuh neh-SAHNSS")
(For two) people	(Pour deux) personnes ("Poor deuh") ("pehr-SUN")
A pharmacist	Un pharmacien ("Anh fahr-mah-see-EHNH")
A pharmacy	Une pharmacie ("Eywn fahr-mah-SEE")
Please	S'il vous plaît ("See voo pleh")
(It was my) pleasure	(C'était mon) plaisir ("Seh-teh moanh pleh-ZEER")
Police	Police ("Poah-LEES")
Police station	Poste de police ("Pust deuh Poah-LEES")
Postcards	Cartes postales (Kahrt poahs-TAHLL")
The Post Office	La Poste ("Pust")
(A) priest	(Un) prêtre ("Anh prehtr")

R

(A) raincoat	(Un) imperméable ("Anh am-pehr-mee-AHBL")
It's raining	Il pleut ("pleuh")
Rare (meat)	Seignant ("Senh-YAHNH")
To rent __	Louer __ ("Loo-AY")
(To make) reservations	(Faire des) réservations ("Fehr deh") ("ray-zehr-vah-see-OANH")
(To the) right	(A) droîte ("Ah") ("drawtt")

S

A scarf	Une écharpe ("Ewn eh-SHARP")
To send	Envoyer ("Ahn-vwah-YAY")
She	Elle ("Ell")
The shirt	La chemise ("Lah sheh-MEEZ")
(These) shoes	(Ces) chaussures ("Ceh") ("shoah-SYEWRE")
(On the) side	(A coté) (Ah koah-TAY")
Sir (male); Mister	Monsieur ("M'SYEUH")
(I take) size __	(Je porte) du __ ("Zheh poahrt") ("dyew"__)
A slip (garment)	Un jupon ("Anh zhew-POANH")
Slowly	Lentement ("Lawnhtt-MAWNH")
It's snowing	Il neige ("Eel nehzh")
(Some) socks	(Des) chausettes ("Deh shoah-SET")
(Do you) speak ___	Parlez-vous ___ ("Pahr-leh-VOO" ___)
A spoon	Une cuillère ("Yewn kwee-EHYR")
(A stage) show (or play)	(Un) pièce ("Anh pee-EHSS")
The stairs	L'escalier ("Less-kahl-YAY")
(Some) stamps	Des timbres ("Deh TAMBRR")
The station (train)	La gare ("Lah gahr")
The station (taxi)	La station ("Lah stah-see-OANH")

Stop	Arrêtez ("Ah-reh-TAY")
Straight	Tout droit ("Too dwah")
A Street	Une rue ("Ewn"ryew")
Street-level floor (in store)	Rez-de-chaussée ("Reh-duh-shoah-SAY")
(A) store	(Un) magasin ("Anh") ("mah-gah-ZANH")
Suburbs	Banlieue ("Bahn-lee-EUH")
The subway (Métro)	Le Métro ("Leuh Meh-TRWOAH")
(Over) there	Là ("Lah")

T

Table	Table ("Tah-bl")
Taxi	Taxi ("Tahk-SEE")
Telephone	Téléphone ("Teh-leh-FUN")
To telephone	Téléphoner ("Teh-leh-fun-AY")
Thank you (very much)	Merci (beaucoup) ("Mehr-SEE") ("boah-KOO")
Theater (stage)	Théâtre ("Teh-AHT-r")
(Movie) theatre	Cinéma ("See-neh-MAH")
There it is	Voilà ("Vwah-LAH")

They
  Masc. or both
  Fem.
	Ils ("Eel")
	Elles ("Ell")

Thief	Voleur ("Voah-LEUHR")
(A) ticket	(Un) billet ("Anh") ("bee-YAY")

To OR in...

Boston	A Boston ("Ah Boahs-TUN")
Canada	Au Canada ("Oah Kah-nah-DAH")
Florida	En Floride ("Awnh Floah-REED")
France	En France ("Awnh FRAWNHSS")
London	A Londres ("Ah Loahndr")
Massachusetts	A Massachusetts ("Ah Mah-sah-chew-SETTS")
New York	A New York ("Ah New YORK")
Paris	A Paris ("Ah Pah-REE")
Provence	En Provence ("Awnh Proah-VAWNHSS")
U.S.	Aux Etats Unis ("Oah-zay-tah-zyew-NEE")
Today	Aujourd'hui ("Oh-zhoor-DWEE")

Tomorrow	Demain ("Deuh-MANH")
Toilet / Women / Men	Les toilettes ("twah-LETT") Dames "Dahm") / Hommes ("Umm")
The train	Le train ("Leuh trehn")
A trip	Un voyage ("Anh vwahy-AHZH")

U

(An) umbrella	(Une) parapluie ("Eywn pah-rah-plew-EE")
Under	Sous ("Soo")
Undercooked	Pas assez cuit ("Pahz ahs-say KWEE")
I understand	Je comprends ("Zheh koahm-PRAWNH")
I don't understand	Je ne comprends (pas) ("Zheh nuh kohm-prawnh PAH")
Some underwear	Des sous-vêtements ("Deh soo-vet-MAWNH")
Upstairs	En haut ("Awnh OH")

V

Vacation	Vacances ("Vah-CAHNSS") OR Holiday ("Oah-lee-DAY")

W

Waiter	Monsieur ("M'syeuh")
Waitress	Madame ("Mah-DAHM")
A wallet	Un portefeuille ("Anh por-teh-FEUHYEE")
Watch out!	Attention! ("Ah-tahn-see-OANH")
(Some) water (plain)	(De) l'eau non-gazeuse("Deh") ("loah noanh gah-ZEUHZ") OR (De) l'eau nature ("Deh") ("loah nah-TYEUR")
(Some) water (sparkling)	(De) l'eau gazeuse("Deh") ("loah gah-ZEUHZ")
We	Nous ("Noo")
(It's) bad (weather)	Il fait mauvais ("Eel feh moah-VEH")
(It's) good (weather)	(Il fait) beau ("Eel feh BOAH")
Week	Semaine ("Seh-MEHN")

(You're) welcome	De rien ("Deuh ree-ANH") **or** (a cooler way) Je vous en pris ("Zheh VOOZ awnh-PREE")
(I'm) well	(Je vais) trés bien ("Zheh veh tray bee-ANH")
	OR Ça va ("Sah VAH")
Well-done (steak)	Bien cuit ("Byangh KWEE")
Where is...?	Où se trouve...? ("Ooh seh TRWOOV"...)
(It's) windy	(Il y a) du vent ("Eel yah dyew VAWNH")
The wine list	La liste des vins ("Lah leest deh VANGH")

Y

Year	Année ("Ah-NAY")
Yes	Oui ("Wee")
Yesterday	Hier ("Ee-EHR")
You	Vous ("Voo")

Numbers 1-50

0	Zero ("Zeh-ROH")
1	Un ("Anh")
2	Deux ("Deuh")
3	Trois ("Twah")
4	Quartre ("Kahtr")
5	Cinq ("Sank")
6	Six ("Sees")
7	Sept ("Set")
8	Huit ("Wheet")
9	Neuf ("Neuhf")
10	Dix ("Dees")
11	Onze ("Oanhz")
12	Douze ("Dooz")
13	Treize ("Trehz")
14	Quartorze ("Kah-TOARZ")
15	Quinze ("Kanhz")
16	Seize ("Sehz")
17	Dix-sept ("Dee-SET")
18	Dix-huit ("Dees-WHEET")
19	Dix-neuf ("Dees-NEUHF")
20	Vingt ("Vanh")
21	Vingt-et-un ("Vanh-teh-ANH")
22	Vingt-deux ("Vanht-DEUH")
30	Trente ("Trawnht")
31	Trente-et-un ("Trawnh-teh-ANH")
32	Trente-deux ("Trawnht-DEUH")
40	Quarante ("Kah-RAWHNT")
41	Quarante-et-un ("Kah-RAWHN-teh-ANH")
42	Quarante-deux ("Kah-RAWHNT-DEUX
50	Cinquante ("Sank-AWHNT")

Numbers 51 and Higher

51	Cinquante-et-un ("Sank-AWHN-teh-ANH")
52	Cinquante-deux ("Sank-AHNT-DEUH")
60	Soixante ("Swah-ZAHNT")
61	Soixante-et-un ("Swah-ZAHN-teh-ANH")
62	Soixante-deux "(Swah-ZAHNT-DEUH")
70	Soixante-dix ("Swah-ZAHNT-DEESS")
71	Soixante-onze ("Swah-ZAHNT-OANHZ")
72	Soixante-douze ("Swah-ZAHNT-DOOZ")
80	Quartre-vingt ("Kahtr-VANH")
81	Quatre-vingt-et-un ("Kahtr-VANH-teh-ANH")
82	Quatre-vingt-deux ("Kahtr-VANH-DEUH")
90	Quatre-vingt-dix ("Kartr-VANH-DEES")
91	Quartre-vingt-onze ("Kartr-VAHNT-OANHZ")
92	Quartre-vingt-douze ("Kahtr-VANGT-DOOZ")
100	Cent ("Sawnh")
101	Cent-et-un ("Sawnh-teh-ANH")
102	Cent-deux ("Sawnt-DEUH")
200	Deux cent ("Deuh SAWNH")
500	Cinq cent ("Sank SAWNH")
1,000	Mil ("Meel")
2006	Deux mil six ("Deuh meel sees")
2007	Deux mil sept ("Deuh meel set")
2008	Deux mil huit ("Deuh meel wheet")
2009	Deux mil neuf ("Deuh meel neuhf")
2010	Deux mil dix ("Deuh meel dees")
1,000,000	Un million ("Unh meel-YOANH")

Days of the Week

Sunday	Dimanche ("Dee-MAHNSH")
Monday	Lundi ("Luhn-DEE")
Tuesday	Mardi ("Mahr-DEE")
Wednesday	Mercredi ("Mehr-creh-DEE")
Thursday	Jeudi ("Zhuh-DEE")
Friday	Vendredi ("Vahn-druh-DEE")
Saturday	Samedi ("Sahm-DEE")

Times of Day

One o'clock	Une heure ("Eywn euhr")
Noon	Midi ("Mee-DEE")
Midnight	Minuit ("Mee-NWEE")
Quarter past three	Trois heures et quart ("Twah-zeuhr eh kahr")
Half past seven	Sept heures et demie ("Set-euhr eh deuh-MEE")
Ten minutes past eleven	Onze heures dix ("Oanh-zeuhr dees")
Quarter of ten	Dix heures moins le quart ("Dee-ZEUHR mwanh leuh kahr")

Getting around Paris

Paris has a full complement of transportation options. For the most part, it's a flat, wonderful walking city (While walking your feet off, watch for dog "deposits" on sidewalks.) Private coin-operated public toilets are scattered in green and white booths throughout Paris— usually near intersections of major thoroughfares.

Skating and Biking

In-line skating is big in Paris. Each Friday at 10P, many STRONG in-line skaters gather in front of Gare Montparnasse for the free "Pari Roller," which snakes through Paris on a different 30-mile route each week. Info: (0)1 43 36 89 81. A less taxing, skate begins at 2:30P each Sunday in the Place de la Bastille. Info: (0)1.44.54.07.44.

Some rental locations for in-line skates ("patins à roulettes"):
Bike 'N Roller; 38, rue Fabert, Esplanade des Invalides (7th Arr.); (0)1.45.50.38.27
Nomades Roller Shop; 37 Boulevard Bourbon (4th Arr.) (0)1.44.54.07.44

Paris offers more than 100 miles of dedicated lanes for bicycling. "Paris Rando Vélo" is a Friday night bicycle expedition through the streets of Paris. Riders meet at l'Hôtel de Ville at 9:30P. About 20,000 bicycles are available for 24/7 rental from Paris Vélib at 1,450 self-serve kiosks throughout the city. There is a refundable deposit of 150€. No charge first half hour; 1€ next 30 minutes; 2€ next 30 minutes; then 4€ per 30 minutes. Less expensive are subscriptions for one day (€1), one week (€5), or one year (€29). Return the bicycle to any kiosk. Kiosks are no more than 350 meters apart. Check bikes over carefully before renting. www.velib.paris.fr (Click on "Download," upper right of site, for English PDF.) (0)1.30.79.79.30.

Tip: Officially, "smart" cards must be used to rent from Vélib Paris. But our American Express Gold Card worked just fine.

Taxis

When we're dressed up, venturing into questionable areas, fatigued, setting out on a complex journey, in a mood to be pampered, or returning to our hotel late at night, we take a taxi.

Serving 15,500 Parisian taxis are 121 taxi stations. It costs less to take a taxi at a taxi station than to phone. One telephone number now accesses all taxi companies: **01.45.30.30.30.** A few of the leading taxi companies: Taxis G7 (has some handicapped-accessible vehicles—see page 89); Taxis Bleus; Alpha Taxis

Tip: Cruising taxis are not supposed to pick up passengers within 50 meters (about 165 feet) of a taxi station. If an empty taxi passes you, it's likely there is a taxi station within sight. (Drivers may conveniently relax the rule during slow periods.) Taxi stations are designated by dark blue signs marked "TAXI."

Tip: A taxi driver may appreciate an immediate reference to the arrondissement you want. Say, "Au" ("Owe")—which means "To the _____," followed by the arrondissement number (you need not say the word "Arrondissement"), then the address. The correct "overture" for each of the 20 arrondissements is scripted below:

Right Bank:
To the 1st: "Au Premier" ("Owe Pruhm-YEH")
To the 2nd: "Au Deuxième" ("Owe Duhz-YEHM")
To the 3rd: "Au Troisième" ("Owe Twahz-YEHM")
To the 4th: "Au Quartrième" ("Owe Kah-trwee-YEHM")
To the 8th: "Au Huitième" ("Owe Wheet-YEHM")
To the 9th: "Au Neuvième" ("Owe Nuhv-YEHM")
To the 10th: "Au Dixième" ("Owe Deez-YEHM")
To the 11th: "A l'Onzième" ("Ah l'oanh-zee-YEHM")
To the 12th: "Au Douzième" ("Owe Dooz-YEHM")
To the 16th: "Au Sixième" ("Owe Seez-YEHM")
To the 17th: "Au Dix-septième" ("Owe Dee-set-YEHM")
To the 18th: "Au Dix-huitième" ("Owe Dees-wheet-YEHM")
To the 19th: "Au Dix-neuvième" ("Owe Dees-neuhv-YEHM")
To the 20th: "Au Vingtième" ("Owe Vanht-YEHM")

Left Bank:
To the 5th: "Au Cinquième" ("Owe Sank-YEHM")
To the 6th: "Au Sixième" ("Owe Seez-YEHM")
To the 7th: "Au Septième" ("Owe Set-YEHM")
To the 13th: "Au Treizième ("Owe Treh-zee-YEHM")
To the 14th: "Au Quatorzième" ("Owe Kah-toarz-YEHM")
To the 15th: "Au Cinquième" ("Owe Sank-YEHM")

After this preamble, quickly give the number and street: "Numéro ("New-meh-WROAH") ____, rue _____." If you have difficulty pronouncing a street name, write it down and show it to the driver, or use the phonetic spelling (For phonetic pronunciation, see pages 50 (letters) and 67 (numbers).

Fares are highest during the hours of 7P-7A and between Paris and the airports. Gratuity: 15%-20%.

A list of taxi stations (with locations and telephone numbers) by arrondissement follows.

List of Taxi Stations

1st Arrondissement:
Place André Malraux 01.42.60.61.40
Place du Châtelet 01.42.33.20.99
Métro Concorde 01.42.61.67.60

2nd Arrondissement:
Place de l'Opéra 01.47.42.75.75

3d Arrondissement:
Métro Rambuteau 01.42.72.00.00
Square du Temple 01.42.78.00.00

4th Arrondissement:
Métro Saint-Paul 01.48.87.49.39

5th Arrondissement:
Place Edmond Rostand 01.46.33.00.00
Pont de la Tournelle 01.43.25.92.99
Place des Gobelins 01.43.31.00.00
Place Monge 01.45.87.15.95
Place Saint-Michel 01.43.29.63.66
Place Maubert 01.46.34.10.32

6th Arrondissement:
Place Henri Mondor 01.43.26.00.00
Métro Port Royal 01.43.54.74.37
Place du 18 juin 1940 01.42.22.13.13
Métro Mabillon 01.43.29.00.00
Saint-Germain des Prés (church) 01.42.22.00.00
Place Alphonse Deville 01.45.48.84.75

List of Taxi Stations (Continued)

7th Arrondissement:
Tour Eiffel 01.45.55.85.41
Place de l'Ecole Militaire 01.47.05.00.00
Métro Solférino 01.45.55.00.00
Place de la Résistance 01.47.05.66.86
Place Léon-Paul Fargue 01.45.67.00.00
Métro Bac 01.42.22.49.64
Métro Latour-Maubourg 01.45.55.78.52
27, blvd. Latour-Maubourg 01.45.51.76.76
Place du Géneral Gouraud 01.47.05.06.89

8th Arrondissement:
Place de la Madeleine 01.45.61.00.00
1, avenue de Friedland 01.42.56.29.00
Rd-Pt des Champs-Elysée 01.47.63.00.00
Place des Ternes 01.40.70.96.04
Place de l'Alma 01.47.42.54.73
Place Saint-Augustin 01.45.62.00.00
Place Rio de Janeiro 01.48.78.00.00

9th Arrondissement:
Square de Montholon 01.48.78.00.00
Place d'Estienne-d'Orves 01.48.74.00.00
Métro Richelieu-Drouot 01.42.46.00.00
2, rue Fléchier 01.42.81.12.24

10th Arrondissement
Place de la République 01.43.55.92.64

11th Arrondissement:
Métro Goncourt 01.42.03.00.00
Place de la République 01.43.55.92.64
Faidherbe-Chaligny 01.43.72.00.00
Place Léon Blum 01.43.79.00.00

12th Arrondissement:
Place de la Bastille 01.43.47.03.32
Porte Dorée 01.46.28.00.00
Place Felix Eboué 01.43.43.00.00
Place de la Nation 01.43.73.29.58
Hôpital Trousseau 01.44.87.95.94

List of Taxi Stations (Continued)

13th Arrondissement:
Porte de Choisy 01 45 85 40 00
1, place Pinel 01 45 86 00 00
Carrefour Patay-Tolbiac 01 45 83 00 00
Métro Glacière 01 45 80 00 00
Porte d'Italie 01 45 86 00 44

14th Arrondissement:
Porte de Vanves 01.45.39.87.33
Métro Plaisance 01.45.41.66.00
Place Denfert-Rochereau 01.43.35.00.00
Place Victor Basch 01.45.45.00.00
1, Avenue Reille 01.45.89.05.71
Porte d'Orléans 01.45.40.52.05

15th Arrondissement:
Métro La Motte-Piquet Grenelle 01.45.66.00.00
252, rue Vaugirard 01.48.42.00.00
Place Charles-Michel 01.45.78.20.00
Place Henri Queuille 01.47.34.00.00
Métro Convention 01.42.50.00.00
Porte de Versailles 01.48.28.00.00
Place Balard 01.45.54.01.89
Place de Breteuil 01.45.66.70.17
44, avenue Félix Faure 01.40. 60.08.37

16th Arrondissement:
Métro La Muette 01.42.88.00.00
Porte Dauphine 01.45.53.00.00
Place Jean-Lorrain 01.45.27.00.00
Gare Henri Martin 01.45.04.00.00
Place d'Auteuil 01.46.51.14.61
Place du Trocadéro 01.47.27.00.00
Métro Passy 01.45.20.00.00
Porte de St-Cloud 01.46.51.60.40
Maison de la Radio 01.42.24.99.99
23, blvd Exelmans 01.45.25.93.91
Porte Molitor 01.46.51.19.19
Place Clément Ader 01.45.24.56.17
Métro Jasmin 01.45.25.13.13
Avenue Victor Hugo/Etoile 01.45.01.85.24
Place d'Iéna 01.40.70.00.36
Place Barcelone 01.45.24.11.11
Place Victor Hugo 01.45.53.00.11

List of Taxi Stations (Continued)

17th Arrondissement:
Métro Brochant 01.46.27.00.00
Place du Maréchal Juin 01.42.27.00.00
Métro Villiers 01.46..22.00.00
Pte de Champerret 01.47.66.22.77
Porte d'Asnières 01.43.80.00.00
Mairie Annexe 01.43.87.00.00
Porte de Clichy 01.46.27.90.06
Porte de Saint-Ouen 01.42.63.00.00
Place de Clichy 01.42.85.00.00

18th Arrondissement:
Place du Tertre 01.42.59.00.00
Place de la Chapelle 01.42.05.49.10
Métro Guy Moquet 01.42.28.00.00
Place Jules Joffrin 01.46.06.00.00
Pont Caulincourt 01.42.54.00.00
Porte de Clignancourt 01.42.58.00.00
Métro Château Rouge 01.42.52.00.00
Place Blanche 01.42.57.00.00
Lamark/Caulincourt 01.42.55.00.00
Damrémont/Ordener 01.42.54.59.00
Porte de la Chapelle 01.42.09.65.52
Porte d'Aubervilliers 01.40.36.08.86

19th Arrondissement:
34, rue de Laumière 01.42.06.00.00
Place du Colonel Fabien 01.42.03.41.50
Eglise de Belleville 01.42.08.42.66
Porte de Pantin 01.42.41.00.62
Porte de la Villette 01..40.34.64.00
Porte des Lilas 01.42.02.71.40
Métro Botzaris 01.42.06.01.32
Métro Stalingrad 01.40.34.00.00
67, rue de Flandre 01.40.35.28.27

20th Arrondissement:
Métro Père LaChaise 01.48.05.92.12
Porte de Montreuil 01.43.70.00.00
Place Gambetta 01.46.36.00.00
Métro Pyrénées 01.43.49.10.00
Métro Ménilmontant 01.43.55.64.00

Public Transportation and the Métro

The public transportation system (the R.A.T.P.) is headed by the famous Métro (subway). The system includes three elements, all of which use the same tickets.

A system of 250 bus ("autobus") lines blankets the city and suburbs from 6:30A to 10:30P. Buses with one- or two-digit numbers serve the interior city, while buses with three-digit numbers serve the suburbs. Buses can be slow but have been speeded up by many special bus lanes. Buses afford a slow-motion view of Parisian life. A list of bus lines appears in *Paris par Arrondissement* (see page 170).

R.E.R. trains go to the suburbs ("banlieue"). Each of the five lines (identified by the letters A, B, C, D, E) has forks, which result in the equivalent of more than 20 "sub-lines."

You'll probably be primarily using the Métro (subway), which crisscrosses the city and close-in suburbs over 131 miles of track and upwards of 300 stations. Transfers between lines are available at about 30% of the stations. The 14 lines are identified by numbers. Two of the 14 split into two forks, creating 16 lines for all intents and purposes. Some stations serve both the Métro and the R.E.R.

The Métro is clean, efficient enjoyable transportation in Paris. Where else can patrons experience live classical, popular, or traditional musical performances in a subway? Many station entrances feature beautiful "dragonfly" iron sculptures of Hector Guimard.

Some stations have personalities of their own. For example, the Louvre station walls look much like the inside of a museum, with many works of sculpture set into the walls.

Metro stations are usually designated, on maps and signs, by Ⓜ .

For details on Métro lines, see the list beginning on page 78.

Some Métro facts:
- Métro trains run from 5:30A until around 12:45A. Trains arrive about every 5-8 minutes, averaging 2-3 minutes from station to station.

- Métro lines are named for their first and last stations. Signs throughout a station often precede the name of the line with the word "Direction___," indicating whether the train will be traveling in the direction of the first or last station on the line. For example, "DIRECTION CHATELET."

- One station may serve multiple lines. As a train enters your station, check the number and direction on the first car to ensure that you have the correct line and the proper direction.

- See the next two pages for ticket purchasing options. Métro stations use ticket-taking turnstiles. Insert the ticket in the nearer slot, face up or face down. It will be returned to you via the second slot (with a date stamp and hash marks indicating that it's now canceled) via the second slot. Retrieve the ticket, and push through the turnstile.

Tip: Keep your canceled ticket. Métro inspectors may ask for proof of purchase at any time; you may be fined if you can't comply.   (2) One ticket serves you all the way through transfers en route to your final destination.

- Once you exit a station, you may not use the same ticket to transfer to another Métro line. Make the connection without first exiting the station.

- Signage: "Renseignements" means a *source* of information. But one *asks* for "directions" (dee-rehk-see OANH). "Sortie" means exit. "Correspondence" refers to a connection between two lines.

- Most Métro doors open only when someone (inside or outside the train) twists a door handle or pushes a button on or by the door.

- The Métro can involve a lot of stairs and corridors. Some of the major stations have escalators or elevators to the street, and that number is slowly growing. Watch out for pickpockets on escalators (see pages 93-94).

- To reach a Métro customer care representative between 7 am and 9 pm Monday-Friday and between 9 am and 5 pm on Saturday, Sunday and bank holidays, telephone this abbreviated number from Paris: 32.46. Calls cost 34 centimes per minute. From the U.S., dial 011.33.8.92.69.32.46.

You have numerous options for purchasing tickets for the Métro. All may be also used on buses or the R.E.R. Quoted prices (as of this writing) are for the least expensive alternatives, usually involving zones 1-2 or 1-3, which will get you anywhere within the 20 arrondissements of Paris. Travel to more distant zones (e.g. Versailles or Disneyland) involve higher costs.

• **An individual ticket,** which may be purchased at a Métro station for €1.60, allows unlimited connections until you exit a station. To purchase one ticket, say "Un billet" ("Anh bee-YEH").

• A **Carnet** ("Kahr-NEH") is a discount book of 10 individual Métro tickets. available at Métro stations and tobacconist shops ("Tabac") for €11.40. The tickets in a carnet may be divided among any number of people. This is a good option if you're intending to use the Métro only occasionally or if you don't have a clue about how you'll be traveling around the city most often.

• A **Mobilis** ("Moah-bee-LEES") pass covers unlimited Métro travel for one day for one person, @ €5.90 or a weekly pass @ €14. It's available at Métro stations. This is primarily for people who plan many Métro trips in a single day or week and don't care about the additional special offers that accompany Le Paris Visite (see below).

• The **Navigo Découverte** ("Day-coo-VEHRT") pass has replaced the Carte Orange. Available at SNCF train stations and Métro stations that have cashiers (mainly the larger stations), Navigo has a built-in microchip, so it's a "swipe" card rather than having to be passed through a turnstile machine. The pass allows unlimited rides on public transportation within Paris (by Métro, bus and RER) for one calendar week (M-S). (For mid-week arrival, it's not a good option.)

You pay €5,00 for the card itself *plus* €16.80 (for zones 1-2) to have the card activated for a week. It also goes to Disneyland, Versailles and Fontainebleau.

The Navigo Découverte pass may be used by only one person, and you're required to provide a small photo of yourself (about the size of a postage stamp). Some Métro stations have photo machines.

• **Le Paris Visite** ("Pah-REE Vee-ZEET") passes are available at all Métro, R.E.R. and SCNF stations, and Services Touristiques de la RATP (Place de la Madeleine in the 8th Arr.). No picture is required. Not available to French citizens.

The option for geographic zones 1-3 gets you unlimited travel anywhere in Central Paris for one day (€9), two days (€14.70, three days (€20), or five days (€28.90). For Paris Visite to be preferable to a Carnet, you should use public transportation at least six times daily (for the five-day option) or nine times daily (for the one-day option). Half price for children ages 4-11; free for younger children.

An option to consider if you will be doing a lot of Métro travel and would like to avail yourself of discounts to 18 selected attractions, museums and one tour. For a list of the discounted venues, go to:

http://goparis.about.com/gi/o.htm?zi=1/XJ&zTi=1&sdn=goparis&cd
n=travel&tm=12&f=12&tt=13&bt=0&bts=0&zu=http%3A//www.ra
tp.info/touristes/index.php%3Flangue%3Den%26rub%3Ddecouvrir
%26cat%3Dparis-visite%26page%3Davantages

Also a good choice if you want to take a train from Paris to either Versailles or Disneyland.

We'd summarize the choices as follows:

Short-term alternatives:

• Carnet/individual billet: Pay-as-you-go; avoids unused tickets

• Le Paris Visite: if traveling 6+ times a day; incl. special offers

Weekly alternative:

• Mobilis: no-frills…unlimited rides €14 per week, starting any day

• Navigo Découverte: unlimited trips within a calendar week beginning Monday and ending Sunday: €21.80 1st Mon.-Sun., €16.80 2nd Mon.-Sun.

Negotiating the Métro

It's important to keep in mind that each Métro line is named for the stations at both ends of that line. The direction in which a train is traveling is identified by the "end-of line" station toward which it is traveling. A train on the Balard/Creteil-Prefecture line would be traveling in "Direction Balard" or "Direction Cretail-Prefecture."

The traditional approach for deciphering the Métro is as follows:

1. On a Paris map, identify (a) your departure location and the Métro station nearest your location and (b) your arrival station and the Métro station nearest that location.

2. Trace all the lines serving your departure station, and determine whether any of them also serves your destination station. If it does, you're in luck and won't have to make a connection. All you have to do is make certain you're going in the right direction.

3. If no direct Métro line exists between departure and destination stations, that's when things get hairy. Now you must trace the various lines serving both your departure and destination station until you find one or more transfers leading to your destination.

Some Métro stations display interactive maps that make it easy. Push buttons indicating your departure and destination stations, and a string of lights highlights the best sequence of Métro lines and connections.

Tracing the multiple colors and shades of Métro lines among the jumble on a map can be unwieldy—especially in dim light or rain. We've developed an alternative approach that we like to call "Plan B."

Plan B

1. On a Paris map, identify (a) your departure location and the Métro station nearest your location and (b) your arrival station and the Métro station nearest that location.

2. Find your departure and destination stations from the list on pages 78-82. Note the number of each line serving your departure station, and repeat the process for your destination station. (Let's assume you'll be traveling from the Blanche station (served by only line 2) to the Bourse station (served by only line 3).

3. Look up line 2 from the list on pages 83-89, and search down the "connections" column for any presence of line 3. Sure enough, the list shows that line 2 and line 3 jointly serve two stations: Vielliers and Père LaChaise. This means that you may transfer from line 2 to line 3 at either of these stations. Just make certain that, before each leg of your journey, you know which direction to take by identifying the terminus station toward which you need to travel.

It is not expected that either the conventional method or the Plan B alternative of dealing with the Métro will appeal to everyone. For example, people who are very visual may prefer the conventional approach, while the analytical mind or poor eyes may gravitate to Plan B.

More than one connection may be necessary to complete a single trip. If it becomes too complex, sometimes there's no alternative but to use the traditional map approach.

Lines Serving Each Métro Station

<u>Métro Stations</u>	<u>Lines</u>
ABBESSES	12
ALESIA	4
ALEXANDRE DUMAS	2
ALMA MARCEAU	9
ANVERS	2
ARTS-ET-METIERS	3, 11
ASSEMBLEE NATIONALE	12
AVRON	2
BARBES ROCHECHOUART	2, 4
BASTILLE	1, 5, 8
BELLEVILLE	2, 11
BERCY	6, 14
BIR HAKEIM	6
BLANCHE	2
BONNE NOUVELLE	8, 9
BOULET MONTREUIL	9
BOUCICAUT	8
BOURSE	3
BREQUET SABIN	5
BUZENTHAL	9
CADET	7
CAMBRONNE	6
CAMPO FORMIO	5
CARDINAL LEMOINE	10
CENSIER DAUBENTON	7
CHAMPS-ELYSEES-CLEMENCEAU	1, 13
CHARLES-DE GAULLE-ETOILE	1, 2, 6
CHARLES MICHELS	10
CHARONNE	9
CHATEAU D'EAU	4
CHATELET	1, 4, 7, 11, 14
CHAUSSEE D'ANTIN	7, 9
CHEMIN VERT	8
CHEVALERET	6
CITE	4

Lines Serving Each Métro Station (Continued)

Métro Stations	Lines
COLONEL FABIAN	2
COMMERCE	8
CONCORDE	1, 8, 12
CONVENTION	12
CORVISART	6
COURCELLES	2
COURONNES	2
DENFERT-ROCHEREAU	4, 6
DUROC	10, 13
ECOLE MILITAIRE	8
EDGAR QUINET	6
EMILE ZOLA	10
ETIENNE MARCEL	4
EXELMANS	9
FAIDHERBE CHALIGNY	8
FALGUIRE	12
FELIX FAURE	8
FILLES DU CALVAIRE	8
FRANKLIN D. ROOSEVELT	1, 9
GAITE	13
GALLIENI	3
GAMBETTA	3
GARE D'AUSTERLITZ	5
GARE DE L'EST	4, 5, 7
GARE DE LYON	1
GARE DU NORD	4, 5
GEORGE V	1
GLACIERE	6
GOBELINS	7
HAVRE CAUMARTIN	3, 9
HOTEL DE VILLE	1, 11
IENA	9
INVALIDES	8, 13
KLEBER	1
JACQUES BONSERGENT5	5

Lines Serving Each Métro Station (Continued)

Métro Stations	Lines
JASMIN	9
JAURES	2, 5, 7b
JAVEL ANDRE CITROEN	10
JUSSIEU	7, 10
LA CHAPELLE	2
LA FOURCHE	13
LAMOTTE-PICQUET	6, 8, 10
LA MUETTE	9
LATOUR MAUBERG	8
LEDRU-ROLLIN	8
LES GOBELINS	7
LES HALLES	4
LIEGE	13
LOURMEL	8
MABILLON	10
MADELEINE	8, 12,14
MAISON BLANCHE	7
MALESHERBES	2
MARAICHERS	9
MAUBERT-MUTUALITE	10
MENILMONTANT	2
MICHEL-ANGE MOLITAR	9
MIROMESNIL	9, 13
MONCEAU	2
MONTPARNASSE BIENVENUE	4, 6, 12, 13
MOUTON-DUVERNET	4
NATION	2, 9
NATIONALE	6
NOTRE-DAME DES CHAMPS	12
NOTRE DAME DE LORETTE	12
OBERKAMPF	5, 9
ODEON	4, 10
OPERA	3, 7, 8
PALAIS-ROYAL	1, 7
PARMENTIER	3

Lines Serving Each Métro Station (Continued)

Métro Stations	Lines
PASTEUR	6, 12
PERE LACHAISE	2, 3
PERNETY	13
PHILIPPE AUGUSTE	2
PIGALLE	2, 12
PLACE DE CLICHY	2, 13
PLACE D'ITALIE	5, 6, 7
PLACE DES FETES	11
PLACE MONGE	7
PLAISANCE	13
POISSONNIER	7
PONT NEUF	7
PORTE DE BAGNOLET	3
PORTE DAUPHINE	2
PORTE DE MONTREUIL	9
PORTE DE ST.-CLOUD	9
PORTE DE VANVES	13
PORTE D'ORLEANS	4
PYRAMIDES	7,14
PYRENEES	11
QUAI DE LA GARE	6
QUAI DE LA RAPES	5
QUARTRE-SEPTEMBRE	3
RAMBUTEAU	11
RANELAGH	9
RASPAIL	4, 6
REAUMUR-SEBASTAPOL	3, 4
RENNES	12
REPUBLIQUE	3, 5, 8, 9, 11
REUILLY DIDEROT	8
RICHARD LENOIR	5
RICHELIEU-DROUOT	8, 9
RIVOLI	1
ROME	2
RUE DE LA POMPE	9

Lines Serving Each Métro Station (Continued)

<u>Métro Stations</u>	<u>Lines</u>
RUE DU BAC	12
RUE MONTMARTRE	8, 9
ST.-AMBROISE	9
ST.-AUGUSTIN	9
ST.-FRANCIS XAVIER	13
ST.-GEORGES	12
ST. GERMAIN DES PRES	4
ST.-LAZARE	3, 12, 13
ST.-MARCEL	5
ST.-MICHEL	4, 10
ST.-PAUL	1
ST.-PHILIPPE DU ROULE	9
ST.-PLACIDE	4
ST.-SULPICE	4
ST.-SEBASTIAN FROISSART	8
SEGUR	10
SENTIER	3
SEVRES-BABYLONE	10, 12
SEVRES-LECOURBE	6
SOLFERINO	12
STALINGRAD	2, 5, 7
STRASBOURG- ST.-DENIS	4, 8, 9
TELEGRAPHE	11
TERNES	2
TRINITE	12
TROCADERO	9
TUILERIES	1
VANEAU	10
VARENNE	13
VAUGIRARD	13
VAVIN	4
VICTOR HUGO	2
VILLERS	2, 3
VOLTAIRE	9
VOLONTAIRES	13

Métro Lines: Stations Served and Connections

(General Compass Directions Abbreviated in Parentheses)

Lines	Connections		Stations
1	LA DEFENSE/CHATEAU DE VINCENNES (W-E)		
	Connections:	2	Charles de Gaulle
		4	Châtelet
		5	Bastille
		6	Charles de Gaulle
		7	Palais-Royal, Châtelet
		8	Bastille, Concorde, Reuilly-Diderot
		9	Franklin D. Roosevelt
		11	Châtelet, Hôtel de Ville
		13	Champs-Elysées-Clemenceau
2	PORTE DAUPHINE / NATION (W-E)		
	Connections:	1	Charles de Gaulle
		3	Villiers, Père LaChaise
		4	Barbes Rochechouart
		5	Stalingrad, Jaurès
		6	Charles de Gaulle
		7B	Jaurès
		9	Nation
		11	Belleville
		12	Pigalle
		13	Place de Clichy
3	PONT DE LEVALLOIS-BECON / GALLIENI (W-E)		
	Connections:	2	Villiers, Pére LaChaise
		3B	Gambetta
		4	G. du Nord, Montparn. Bien., Reaum., Sebast.
		5	République
		7	Opéra
		8	Opéra, République
		9	Havre Caumartin, République
		11	Arts et Métiers, République
		12	St. Lazare
		13	St.-Lazare
3B	GAMBETTA / PORTE DE LILAS (S-N)		
	Connections:	3	Gambetta
		11	Porte de Lilas

Métro Lines: Stations Served and Connections (Cont'd)

<u>Lines</u> <u>Connections</u> <u>Stations</u>

4 PORTE D'ORLEANS/PORTE DE CLINGANCOURT (S-N)

Connections:	1	Châtelet
	2	Barbès Rochechouart
	3	Réaumur-Sebastopol
	5	Gare du Nord, Gare de l'Est
	6	Denfert-Rochereau, Raspail
	7	Châtelet, Gare de l'Est
	8	Strasbourg-St.-Denis
	9	Strasbourg-St.-Denis
	10	Odéon
	11	Châtelet
	12	Montparnasse Bienvenue, Marcadet-Poissonnier
	13	Montparnasse Bienvenue
	14	Châtelet

5 PLACE D'ITALIE / BOBIGNY-PABLO PICASSO (S-N)

Connections:	1	Bastille
	2	Stalingrad, Jaurès
	3	République
	4	Stalingrad
	5	Gare de l'Est
	6	Place d)Italie
	7	Gare de l'Est, Place d'Italie, Stalingrad
	7B	Jaurès
	8	Bastille, République
	9	Oberkampf, République
	10	Gare d'Austerlitz
	11	République

6 CHARLES DE GAULLE - ETOILE / NATION (W-E)

Connections:	1	Charles de Gaulle-Etoile, Nation
	2	Charles de Gaulle-Etoile, Nation, Nation
	4	Denfert-Rochereau, Montpar. Bien., Raspail
	5	Place d'Italie
	7	Place d'Italie
	8	LaMotte-Picquet, Daumesnil
	9	Trocadéro
	10	LaMotte-Picquet
	12	Montparnasse Bienvenue, Pasteur
	13	Montparnasse Bienvenue, Pasteur
	14	Bercy

Métro Lines: Stations Served and Connections (Cont'd)

Lines Connections Station

7 LA COURNEUVE - 8 MAI 1945 /MAIRE D'IVRY VIL.-L. ARAGON (S-N)

Connections:	1	Châtelet, Palais-Royal-Musée de Louvre
	2	Stalingrad
	3	Opéra
	4	Châtelet, Gare de l'Est, Chàteau-Landon
	5	Gare de l'Est, Pl. d'Italie, Stalingrad, Chàt-Landon
	6	Place dItalie
	7B	Louis Blanc
	8	Opéra
	9	Chaussée d'Antin-La Fayette
	10	Jussieu
	11	Châtelet
	14	Châtelet

7B LOUIS BLANC / PRE-ST.-GERVAIS (W-E)

Connections:	2	Jaurès
	5	Jaurès
	7	Louis Blanc
	11	Place des Fêtes

8 BALARD / CRETEIL-PREFECTURE (S-N-S)

Connections:	1	Bastille, Concorde, Reuilly-Diderot
	3	Opéra, République
	4	Strasbourg-St.-Denis
	5	Bastille, République
	6	LaMotte-Picquet, Daumesnil
	7	Opéra
	9	Bonne Nouvelle, République, Richelieu- Drouot, Rue Monmartre, Strasbourg-St.-Denis, Gr. Blvds.
	10	LaMotte-Picquet
	11	République
	12	Madeleine, Concorde
	13	Invalides
	14	Madeleine

9 PONT DE SEVRES / MAIRIE DE MONTREUIL (W-E)

Connections:	1	Franklin D. Roosevelt, Nation
	2	Nation
	3	Havre Caumartin, République
	5	Oberkampf, République
	6	Nation
	7	Chaussée d'Antin
	8	Bonne Nouvelle, République, Richelieu-Drouot, Rue Montmartre, Strasbourg-St.-Denis, Gr. Blvds.
	10	Michel-Ange-Molitor, Michel-Ange-Auteuil
	11	République
	12	Saint-Augustin
	13	Miromesnil, Saint-Augustin
	14	Miromesnil

Métro Lines: Stations Served and Connections (Cont'd)

<u>Lines</u>	<u>Connections</u>	<u>Stations</u>

10 BOULOGNE PONT DE ST. CLOUD/GARE D'AUSTERLITZ (W-E)

Connections:
	4	Odéon
	5	Gare d'Austerlitz
	6	LaMotte-Picquet-Grenelle
	7	Jussieu
	8	LaMotte-Picquet-Grenelle
	12	Sèvres-Babylone
	13	Duroc

11 CHATELET / MAIRIE DES LILAS (W-E)

Connections:
	1	Hôtel de Ville, Châtelet-Avenue Victoria
	2	Belleville
	3	Arts-et-Métiers, République
	3B	Porte de Lilas
	5	République
	7	Châtelet-Avenue Victoria
	7B	Place des Fêtes
	8	République
	9	République
	14	Châtelet-Avenue Victoria

12 MAIRIE D'ISSY / PORTE DE LA CHAPELLE (S-N)

Connections:
	1	Concorde
	2	Pigalle
	3	St.-Lazarre
	4	Montparnasse Bienvenue, Marcadet-Poissonniers
	6	Montparnasse Bienvenue, Pasteur
	8	Madeleine, Concorde
	9	St.-Lazarre
	10	Sèvres-Babylone
	13	Montparnasse Bienvenue, St.-Lazarre
	14	Madeleine, St.-Lazarre

13 CHATILLON-MONTROUGE / ST. DENIS-UNIV. (S-N)

Connections:
	1	Champs-Elysées-Clemenceau
	2	Place de Clichy
	3	St.-Lazare
	4	Montparnasse-Bienvenue
	6	Montparnasse-Bienvenue
	8	Invalides
	9	Miromesnil, St.-Lazare
	10	Duroc, St.-Lazare
	12	Montparnasse Bienvenue, St.-Lazare
	13B	La Fourche
	14	St.-Lazare

13B GABRIEL PERI AS.-GENNEVILLIERS/LA FOURCHE (N-S)

Connections:
	13	La Fourche

Métro Lines: Stations Served and Connections (Cont'd)

Lines	Connections	Stations
14		MADELEINE / BIBLIOTHÈQUE F. MITTERAND (N-S)
	Connections: 1	Châtelet, Gare de Lyon
	3	Pyramides, St.-Lazare
	4	Châtelet
	6	Bercy
	7	Châtelet, Pyramides
	8	Madeleine
	9	St.-Lazare
	11	Châtelet
	12	St.-Lazare, Madeleine
	13	St.-Lazare

The Batobus Shuttle Boat

Except for the period between January 3 and February 4, the Batobus ("Bah-toah-BOOS") shuttle boat on the Seine stops near eight major sites: Eiffel Tower, Musée d'Orsay, St.-Germain-des-Prés, Notre Dame, Jardin des Plantes, Hôtel de Ville, the Louvre, and the Champs Elysées. There's no tour commentary. But it's a pleasant ride; can reduce your walking load, avoids the hassle of Métro connections; and prevents arguments with taxi drivers about "short haul" fares.

Timetable:

February 5-March 18	10:30A-4:30P
March 19-May 27	10:00A-7:00P
May 28-August 29	10:00A-9:30P
August 30-November 3	10:00A-7:00P
November 4-December 25	10:30A-4:30P
December 26-January 2	10:30A-6:30P

You can buy a day pass (€9), 2-day pass (€17), or 5-day pass (€20) and hop on and off as many times as you wish during a given day. (Roughly half-price for children under age 16.) Departures from each stop occur every 15-30 minutes. However, there are often long lines (especially at the Eiffel Tower) that could force you to miss a boat; so this may not be the mode of transportation to take if you're on a tight schedule. (0)8.25.05.01.01 (15 centimes/minute)   www.batobus.com

Sarah C. Dorr and Richard S. Dorr

Being Handicapped in Paris

The French word for "handicapped" is handicapé (masculine) or handicapée (feminine).   In general, Paris is gradually becoming increasingly responsive to the needs of the handicapped.   Larger numbers of public places are handicapped-accessible; many have handicap-accessible restrooms.   At the airport, request a copy of the AeroGuide for disabled travelers in the airport.

Paris has some distance to go as a hospitable place for handicapped people.   There seems to be a concerted effort to discourage vagrants from frequenting the central city, to the extent that officials may have gone overboard in limiting places to sit in public areas other than parks.   Narrow streets and use of sidewalks for restaurant/café terraces may have contributed to the tendency for building facades to be straight up-and-down, with no handy lower window ledges for leaning or sitting.   Moreover, Parisians often like to hug buildings when they walk in their purposeful manner.   And it's easy to feel hurried along by the purposeful strides of crowds.

In general Paris taxi drivers are not anxious to put wheelchairs in their trunks; and they may bypass someone in a wheelchair who is trying to flag a taxi.   We have one friend who is a paraplegic but has a lot of body strength.   He was so enraged at the refusal of one taxi driver that he somehow found a way to throw his wheelchair at the taxi!

Fortunately, the news for the handicapped is not all bad.   In several situations in which we've been temporarily handicapped, we've fared surprisingly well (although it was an ordeal at times).   If you schedule wheelchairs ahead of time through your airline, you'll usually get very good service upon your arrival at a Paris airport.   In fact, we've been "wheelchair-whisked" through the airport and luggage retrieval and right to a taxi door before most of the other passengers on our plane.

For anyone who—though not wheelchair-bound—has problems walking great distances, we feel one piece of equipment is essential. It's a light-weight, three-legged, folding seat—available at golf shops.

For numerous tips on surviving in Paris with a handicap, refer to an excellent article for the handicapped in Paris, written by someone who has obviously gone through the experience. It may be found at: http://www.anamericaninparis.com/Article-Handicapped.html

There's a website listing Paris hotels with handicapped facilities: http://www.france-hotel-guide.com/disabled_travellers.htm

The French term for "a wheelchair" is "un chaise roulant" ("anh shez roo-LAHNH"). Wheelchairs may be rented for roughly €16 per week (or more depending on your specifications) from:

CRF (19th Arron.): (0)1.43.73.98.98
Material Paramedica (6th Arron.): (0)1.43.26.75.00

GIHP provides specially equipped vehicles to transport the disabled: (0)1.45.23.83.50

G7 taxis have special equipment to serve handicapped people. Call the universal taxi line (01.45.30.30.30), ask for the G7 ("Zheh Set") taxi, and request "un taxi pour personnes à mobilité réduite" ("anh tahk-SEE poor pehr-SUN mow-beel-ee-TAY ray-DWEET").

Some museums (including the Louvre) rent out wheelchairs. It's probably wise to call ahead in order to make arrangements.

Communications

France has upgraded its communications resources in recent years.

Telephones

French telephone numbers consist of a city code plus eight digits. The city code for Paris is 01 if you're dialing from Paris and 1 if you're dialing from the U.S. (in which case you also have to precede the 1 with the French country code (33).

If you see a prefix of 05 before an eight-digit number, it's a number that cannot be accessed from outside France. A prefix of 06 denotes a mobile phone. A prefix of 08 precedes a toll-free number.

If you dial Paris directly from the U.S., dial:
    011 (to indicate an international call); then...
    33 (the country code for France); then...
    1 (the city code for Paris); then...
      the eight-digit Paris telephone number

If you dial Paris from within Paris, simply dial 01 followed by the eight-digit telephone number. Thus, throughout this book, phone numbers beginning with "(0)1" mean that you'll dial the "0" if calling from Paris but not if calling from the U.S.

If you're dialing to the U.S. from Paris, coin-operated telephones are difficult to find, being located mainly in a few bars or cafés. Dialing from a hotel room can be expensive.

The only way to use most telephone booths—and the least expensive way to call the U.S. from Paris—is by inserting a Télécarte, (or Carte Téléphonique) which is available at Post Offices, tabacs (tobacco shops), Métro stations, airports, and some newsstands. This card contains either 60 or 120 telephone "units" and costs roughly €8 or €15 respectively. Insert the card when prompted to "introduire votre carte."

To call the U.S. with a Télécarte or from a hotel, dial 00 + 1 (country code for the U.S.) + the U.S. Area Code + the local U.S. number.

Using a U.S. telephone calling card (from a pay phone or a hotel phone) is not difficult and will avoid hotel surcharges. Direct-dial instructions:

ATT: Dial 0-800-99-0011; (prompt) area/number; (prompt) calling card number
Verizon: Dial 0-800-99-2016; 634; follow voice prompts
Sprint: Dial 0-800-99-0087; follow voice prompts
MCI: Dial 0-800-99-0019; PIN; 1+area code/number

If you want to use your cell phone in Paris, call your provider to determine how to make the adaptation. Alternatively, you may rent a cell phone in Paris (in fact, they'll probably deliver it to your hotel quite quickly) from Rent A Cell Express: (0)1.53.93.78.00 or Euro Exaphone: (0)1.44.09.77.78.

Tip: If you hear "Ne Quittez Pas" ("Neh kee-TAY Pah") during a phone conversation, it means "Hold the line." The French sometimes say it so fast that "Quittez" is all you hear. Don't hang up as Dick did the first eight times.

For telephone information in Paris, dial 12; for an operator, dial 10.

Paris telephone books have two versions: White Pages (Pages Blanches) and Yellow Pages (Pages Jaunes), just as in the U.S.

Mail

The French postal system has the same name as an individual post office: "La Poste." Stamps (timbres, pronounced "tambrr") are available at Tabac shops or Post Offices (most of which also offer fax service). The *Plan de Paris par Arrondissement et Communes de Banlieue* (see reference on page 170) contains a list of Post Offices.

The main Post Office in Paris is located at 52, rue de Louvre in the 1st Arrondissement. It is the only European Post Office that is open 24 hours a day, 365 days a year. The 24-hour telephone number of the main Post Office: (0)1.40.28.20.00.

Newspapers

Paris has had news kiosks since 1720. The word for newspaper is "Journal" (zhoor-NAHL). Kiosks, all over the place, sell two English-language dailies: *The International Herald Tribune* (Monday-Saturday) and *USA Today* (Monday-Friday). But the fairly limited supply tends to disappear by mid-morning. There's usually a one-day lag in the news that's printed. *Paris Voice* is a bi-monthly magazine that bills itself as "the magazine for English-speaking Parisians."

The two principal Paris newspapers are the French-language *Le Monde* and *Le Figaro*.

Entertainment Information

For information on entertainment, two French-language publications appear on newsstands each Wednesday: *L'Officiel des Spectacles* and *Pariscope*. If you have difficulty deciphering them, the people at your hotel front desk will help. Two English-language publications, *Paris Boulevard* and *Time Out Paris*, are published periodically.

Tip: Several ticket agencies serve Paris. The one we've found most convenient is in the basement of the department store, Galéries Lafayette (see page 121), near the Book Department.

Safety

You're on a Métro escalator, about to ascend to the Champs Elysées. A young adult ahead of you starts juggling an article—perhaps a cigarette lighter—and happens to drop it on the grating at the top of the ascent. He stoops to retrieve it; you trip over him; and his two accomplices behind you fall on the pile. This is just one of several devices used by pickpockets, who have targeted us four times in Paris (via different schemes) without success. As in any big city, you should be on guard. If you're alert for this ploy, you can squeeze by the first thief and "accidentally" give him a kick for his trouble.

Another trick involves someone wedging in with you as you exit the narrow doors or turnstile of a Métro station. As you struggle against this shocking affront, his accomplice picks your pocket from behind.

Tip: In general, Parisians are polite, physically agile, and private. When a stranger in Paris appears clumsy, aggressive, rude, or persistently overly-helpful, get suspicious in a hurry. Grab your wallet or pocketbook immediately, and escape quickly.

When the doors of a Métro car are about to close, protect your wallet or pocketbook carefully. Don't keep wallets in your hip pocket. Women should clutch their handbags even if a bag has a shoulder strap, because thieves will sometimes cut the strap. A thief may grab a valuable and squeeze to the other side of the Métro door just as it closes. Or packs of young children may cluster around you, while one attempts to pick your pocket in the confusion. And thieves just love backpacks. Always be aware of what's going on around you.

Gypsy women with children often cruise the sidewalk on the Right Bank above the Seine or near the Eiffel Tower, seeking tourist couples. The kids panhandle the male of the duo, maneuvering him away from his female companion. The mother pleads with the woman for money, getting ever-closer until her hand somehow winds up in the victim's pocketbook. If you're a couple approached by a stranger, refuse to be separated. Individual gypsies work the Tuileries Gardens near the Louvre. If a stranger (especially in a long dress) asks whether you speak English, shake your head, "No," and say nothing.

Tip: Try to use maps, guidebooks and cameras inconspicuously, because they identify you as a tourist—therefore a juicy "mark."

In railway stations, if someone claims to be an "inspector" or asks to see your ticket or tries to "help" you with a stubborn ticket-dispensing machine, be suspicious and ask for identification. Otherwise, you may never see your ticket again.

TIP: The French word for thief is voleur ("voah-LEUHR"); the word for police is "police; " and loud yelling is a universal alarm.

The **first rule** to avoid petty theft is not to look conspicuously like a tourist. A fanny pack and white sneakers are like "ROB ME" neon signs. And, if you want to seal your fate, pull out a Paris map or guidebook and pore over it in the middle of a crowd.

The **second rule** is constantly to be aware of what's going on around you. Any disturbance; anyone leaning against you; someone trying to "give" you anything; any hint of impoliteness…all of these things should instantly put you on the alert.

The **third rule** is to cover your goodies. A lightweight, medium-length topcoat is perfect for (a) guarding against sudden rain and (b) covering inviting clothes pockets. Consider carrying one, even in warm weather, and slip it on when you're entering suspicious territory.

Dick had a French tutor for a while, and the first French words the tutor taught him involved a physically impossible act, which would be unprintable here. Asked why he had picked that term, he said, "You'll need it in Paris some day." Much later, two thieves tried the "Métro turnstile wedgie" gambit. Dick felt a hand vainly trying to cram itself into his back pocket, and he spun around and whacked the attempted thief, screaming this epithet at him. The guy started to run down an empty Métro corridor, and Dick took off after him, still yelling the very nasty words. Suddenly, Dick realized he and the guy were alone in that corridor, and he had no idea whether the thief might be armed; so he stopped giving chase, very thankful that this jerk, like virtually all Parisian sneak thieves, was basically a coward. So the **fourth rule** is not to let your emotions run away with you; play it smart.

Potpourri of Helpful Hints

Following are some suggestions covering a variety of situations.

Babysitting

Experienced English-speaking babysitters are available through three reliable agencies: Kid Service: tel. (0)1.42.61.90.00); Baby-sitting service: tel. (0)1.46.37.51.42); Ababa: tel. (0)1:45.49.46.46 They'll generally charge €4 to €5 per hour, with a three-hour minimum.

Gratuities

Most eating places add a 15% gratuity on the bill, which specifies "Service compris" If unsure as to whether the gratuity is included, ask: "Service compris? ("Sehr-VEES koahm-PREE?"). If the service warrants, consider leaving an additional one to five per cent in cash.

Tip taxi drivers at least 10% (we prefer 20%), and be prepared to pay roughly €1 extra per piece of luggage. A hotel porter should receive at least €1 per bag; a housekeeper at least €1 per person per day. A concierge might merit a gratuity from €10 to €50, depending on how helpful (s)he has been. A coat-check person should get €1 per coat.

When someone provides a service that's not common in the U.S., such as handing out towels in a bathroom, offer a gratuity of 25 centimes to €1. A theatre usher should receive 50 centimes to €1. If you're in doubt about gratuities, follow the guidelines you'd observe in the U.S.

Lost Articles

• Phone numbers to call **if your credit cards are lost or pilfered**:

  American Express (stolen card): (0)1.47.77.70.00
  VISA: 08.92.70.57.05
  MasterCard: (0)1.45.67.53.53
  Other cards: (0)1.42.77.11.90

• The **Bureau des Objects Trouvées** (found articles), is located at 36, rue des Morillons in the 15th Arrondissement; 08.21.00.25.25.

Kissing

• The face-touching kisses of the French are called "les bises" (lay BEES"). Right cheek to right, then left to left. Some people prefer two "pecks;" others three or four. Sally believes this lip-avoidance approach originated because of the effect of strong French cigarettes on one's breath.

Key Resources

• The **American Hospital** is located at 63, blvd. Victor Hugo in the nearby suburb of Neuilly; (0)1.46.41.25.25

• An **English-language S.O.S. / crisis line**: (0)1.47.21.46.46

• **Ambulance**: dial 15   **Police**: dial 17   **Fire**: dial 18

• For a **doctor**, dial (0)1.47.07.77.77

• For a **dentist**, dial (0)1.43.37.51.00

• An **anti-poison center**: dial (0)1.40.05.48.48

• To reach a **burns center**, dial (0)1.58.41.26.49

• **Pharmacies** are indicated by signs consisting of lit green crosses. Pharmacists are allowed to treat minor wounds. A **24-hour pharmacy** named Pharmacie les Champs is located at 84, av. des Champs-Elysées. Dial (0)1.45.62.02.41

• For **eye care**, dial (0)1.40.92.93.94

Information

The Convention and Visitors Bureau of Paris (Office de Tourisme de des Congrès de Paris) may be reached by telephone at 08.92.68.30.00. Offices are situated in various Paris locations.

American Express Office

If you're a cardholder, the American Express office can be useful in many ways, check-cashing, money transfers, mail pickup, information and advice, card replacements, etc. (11, rue Scribe; Paris 75009 France; Tel. (0)1.47.77.70.00)

Driving

Paris traffic is intense, persistent and quirky. The French tend to flick lights instead of using horns. Drive on the right side. Don't travel in the bus lanes set off by dotted lines; police are very strict about this. Seatbelts are mandatory for all occupants of the car. Breakdown service: (0)1.47.07.99.99.

Parking is nearly impossible; and parking meters (should you be lucky enough to find a vacant one) are closely monitored. If you don't see parking meters, don't assume parking is free. Typically, coin machines—set back from the street—substitute for parking meters. These devices dispense parking vouchers, to be displayed on dashboards, for whatever length of time you purchase.

Sales Taxes

A "value added" sales tax (known as a "TVA" in France) ranges from 5.21% on books to 16.38% on many consumer products. People living outside the European Union (including the U.S.) who spend at least €175 at a single store on the same day are entitled to a refund of 12%-13% (known as a "detaxe") of the TVA on certain items (clothing, shoes, accessories, furnishings). The refund is not for the entire amount of the tax but usually about three-quarters of that amount. Stores are not required to provide the paperwork—they do so on a voluntary basis—and it's a good idea to ask about the availability of a tax refund receipt before making a purchase.

To set the tax refund into motion, ask at the store for a Détaxe Form, which should be stamped by the store. Make certain the paperwork specifies that your refund will be applied to a credit card (even if your purchase was in cash) in order to avoid currency conversion fees when you receive the refund.

For additional information: tel. (0)1.41.61.51.51 or (0)1.42.60.29.29 or http://www.parisescapes.com/paris_department_vat_refund.html

Present the form at the window marked "DETAXE" at the airport for endorsement by customs. (Allow as much as an extra hour for this process due to lines.) You must be carrying the items with you or in your luggage; you may have problems if you have sent them home. The store will later send you the refund in euros or, preferably, will apply it to your credit card so it will automatically be converted into U.S. dollars. Some stores will immediately give you the refund in anticipation that you will submit the required paperwork at the airport.

You can apply for the refund only in the last European Union country you visit on your trip. For example, if you travel to London after Paris, you apply in London—even for Paris purchases. However, you must have your detaxe form stamped by a customs official before leaving the country of purchase even if you will be applying for a refund in another country.

Cleaning Clothes

Laundromats ("laveries") exist—but not many. The French word for laundry detergent is "lessive." Fabric softener is called "soupline."

A place that does your laundry is a blanchisserie.

A dry cleaning establishment is a nettoyage à sec.

We've also seen "Pressing" signs. Same-day or next-day service is rare outside of the luxury hotels.

But What about All those Parisians?

Yes, we've heard the alleged witticism that Paris would be just great if it weren't for all those Parisians. Many first-timers worry that the people of Paris will be cold or rude.

We consistently find that Parisians are very nice—but discriminating, private, selective, and quite cautious around strangers. Once their trust is gained, they can become lifelong friends; and we've been the beneficiaries in numerous cases.

Tourists understandably judge Parisians by those with whom they most frequently interact—service people such as waiters and clerks. Parisian workers from all walks of life identify closely with their jobs, which they take very seriously. Demean, patronize, or ignore a waiter in the course of his duties, and you are seen as attacking his profession as well as his persona.

Many tourists seem to adopt the attitude that money gives them license to subject service people to patronizing, demanding, boorish, loud behavior. This unfortunate situation seems more prevalent on the Right Bank, which—along with its inherent beauty, charm and historical monuments—is a magnet for luxury, affluence, commerce and tourism.

It's on the Right Bank where one is more likely to hear an exasperated tourist exclaim, "These people don't even speak English." (We'll just never get over that one; and, by the way, a large number of Parisians seem to take pride in having learned at least some English.) It's possible that the majority of tourists who return with complaints about Parisian arrogance would benefit from a long look in the mirror.

It's not uncommon for Parisian service people to develop a somewhat detached veneer, which our retired waiter friend, René, describes as a defense mechanism that is occasioned primarily by tourist behavior. Rather than responding by lashing out, Parisians typically become excessively stiff, curt, or even patronizing. It's easy to interpret this facade as pomposity, when it's really a subtle, overly polite rebuke.

In a park, a Parisian becomes the master of the relaxed stroll. In a café, a Parisian's laughter flows easily (though not noisily). However, on the way to work or an errand, a Parisian's gait becomes brisk, the carriage purposeful, the route efficient. Such resolute, task-oriented demeanor undoubtedly contributes to perceptions of Parisian aloofness or even pushiness. It pays to remember that you, not they, are on vacation.

Please don't mistake all of this as an apology for Parisian behavior. No such apology is warranted. We simply want to clarify some of the reasons underlying the idiosyncrasies of Parisian behavior. After all, this book is all about bonding with Paris; and one way to bond with a place is to understand it as fully as possible.

We suggest these guidelines in relating to Parisians:

1. Try to speak at least a little French. Dick will never be a superlative French linguist; but he has consistently found that effort is more important than excellence in gaining cordial acceptance. Refer to pages 45-67 for key words and phrases. We bet you already know a number of them. Our maxim is that bad French is welcomed much more than no French.

2. Be respectful to waiters and clerks, who take a virtual artisan's pride in their jobs. To be treated with disdain is a major affront. Upon entering a small shop, greet the clerk: "Bonjour madame" (or "mademoiselle" if young, or "monsieur"). When leaving, whether or not you've made a purchase, say, "Merci madame" ("mademoiselle," "monsieur"). Greet a waiter or waitress with "Bonjour" BEFORE asking a question or placing an order. ("Bonsoir" in the evening)

3. When shopping, keep in mind that the self-service concept is not as popular in Paris as in the U.S. Don't assume clerks are being pushy when they want to wait on you. They may just be doing their jobs. Je ne fais que regarder ("Zheh neh fay keh reh-gahr-DAY") means "I'm just browsing."

4. When you're dealing with service people, requesting works better than demanding. If you sense you've gone over the line, recoup by adding, "...please" (..."s'il vous plaît"). Opportunistically meeting a waiter's eye is more ultimately effective than an ostentatious summons; they're usually quite attentive. Waiters feel that being the one who pays the bill doesn't give one the license to be dictatorial. Say, "Monsieur" (Sir)—NEVER "Garçon" ("Boy")—in addressing a waiter.

5. If you commit a gaffe, practice self-deprecating humor. Try slapping your forehead and rolling your eyes. It works for Dick, although he does seem to get a lot of headaches.

6. If you feel you're encountering a lot of unwarranted arrogance on the Right Bank, switch banks (so to speak).

7. If you do meet the occasional 24-karat Parisian jerk, ask yourself whether that person might not have a counterpart wherever you live. One loser doesn't necessarily characterize an entire species. Deal with it as you would at home.

Tip: We believe that a smile, ideally accompanied by the word "Bonjour" or "Merçi" is probably the number one social ally of the visitor to Paris.

Traveling alone in Paris

Paris is a fine place for travel, even if you're alone. What a spot to visit a park, enjoy some solitude with a good book, and people-watch!

Meeting people isn't difficult either. But do it intelligently. We feel the best way to meet people is in a ticket line or by sitting at the next table in a restaurant (see two of our experiences on page 40). Proximity encourages conversation and allows you to observe people's companions, hear the language they speak, and pick up clues about their personalities. The fact that they've chosen the same destination as you suggests you have common tastes. The public, happenstance nature of your meeting place contains none of the innuendos of, say, a bar encounter.

We've had female friends who feign neediness when in restaurants, and waiters fall all over them. We'll leave that decision to you.

Many people frequent wine bars or cafés or cyber cafés (see page 29) to meet others. Caution is the watchword. In these settings, we strongly recommend that you focus on people for whom yours is their native language. It may seem less exotic, but it affords you an element of control if you're able to overhear side-conversations or even if you should have need of making your wishes clearly understood. Never get drunk while alone, because that's just an invitation to trouble.

Tips for Women Traveling Alone: Take a taxi, rather than the Métro, late at night. (See pages 68-71 for locations of taxi stations.) In general, at night, stick to places that are filled with people and merriment. For example, we would avoid Montmartre and the surrounding area when it's dark.

The English-language bookstore, Shakespeare & Company (see pages 147-149), is a fine place to meet people, especially at their free tea parties that begin at 4:00 each Sunday.

We have two friends who originally met at the Hermitage Museum in St. Petersburg, Russia. They were both middle-aged products of divorce…the man from Vermont and the woman from Russia. Neither spoke the language of the other, but the woman was with her sister, who spoke a little English. The three had coffee, and Olga and Matt agreed to email one another, which they did for about a year—each with a translator at his/her side. They then agreed to meet in Paris (where else?), and the bond was solidified (which they were somehow able to accomplish without reading this book). To make a long story short, they have now been married for about 10 years; she has become a U.S. citizen; she has learned English, and he has learned a few Russian words; and they now live very nicely in Ecuador (perhaps in order to add Spanish to their list of challenges).

So do not hesitate to visit Paris, whether or not you'll be with someone. Just be careful, and you'll find Paris to be most welcoming, although we're not implying that you'll wind up in wedded bliss like our friends.

Synopsis: Bonding with Paris

- Always have with you: passport (**remember the "90-day rule" on page 13**) plus artificial sweetener, dictionary or phrasebook, umbrella, water, and compact detailed map such as *Paris par Arrondissement.*

- Don't overlook the value of exploring your neighborhood and getting in tune with its unique rhythms and nuances. Identify neighborhood resources. Take time to learn more about the neighborhood where you're living until it becomes the core (but not the geographic limit) of your "personal sanctuary" in Paris.

- Develop a few people-watching vantage points that you may revisit to introduce a little sense of continuity into your visit: the same breakfast place each day; selected cafés; a local park; etc.

- In restaurants, don't be afraid to "cross-table-talk" to neighbors. They may have valuable insights, or you might even strike it rich in the form of a lifelong friendship. What's the potential harm in a tiny social risk, when you consider the possible rewards?

- If little adventures intrigue you, be prepared, vigilant, opportunistic, receptive, observant, spontaneous, adaptable, energetic, outgoing.

- Develop at least a rudimentary familiarity with the language (the 40 "survival terms"—see pages 45-47). Awkward French is much better than none.

- Always be aware of what's going on about you, to reduce the danger of being surprised by sneak thieves—particularly around the Métro. Apparent rudeness should be the signal to be immediately on guard.

- To negotiate the Métro efficiently, consider the approach that appears on page 77.

- To use most phone booths, you'll need a card called Télécarte, (or Carte Téléphonique) available at Post Offices, tabacs (tobacco shops), Métro stations, airports, and some newsstands. Paris telephone numbers have 10 digits, always beginning with 01. However, when you dial Paris from the U.S., omit the initial zero after dialing the direct-dial access number 011 and the country code 33.

- Proud Parisians see all too much objectionable tourist behavior. Be patient. Say, "Bonjour," "Bonsoir," "S'il vous plaît," and "Merci." Address Parisians as "Madame" or "Mademoiselle" or "Monsieur." Request rather than demanding. Be a little self-deprecating when appropriate.

- Don't be afraid to travel alone to Paris. Just use your head, be careful, and consider the other tips we've provided.

- Above all, SMILE, SMILE, SMILE.

On the Town

Because Paris is Paris, you'll likely spend the bulk of your time dining, drinking, sightseeing and shopping. These daily activities will shape many lasting impressions, so they deserve some attention here.

Dining and Drinking Practices in Paris

Eating and drinking places in Paris are differentiated by size, form of ownership, scope of offerings, hours of operation and ambience.

Cafés focus largely on beer, wine and basic cocktails but usually serve breakfast and snacks too. There are more than 7,000 cafés in Paris—about 15% of the number in the late 1800s. Do not confuse cafés with bars, which usually serve only drinks and are often likely to contain noisy pinball machines. Many cafés are closed by 9:00P.

Wine bars primarily serve wine by the glass in an informal setting but also offer basic snacks and lunch items. They generally open by 7:30-8:30 in the morning and close by 9:00 or 10:00P.

Salons de thé ("tay") have sometimes been described as cafés for women. This is probably not as much a gender distinction as it is a commentary on the relative refinement of the salon de thé—part tea room, part coffee shop. The fare consists largely of light meals, cakes and pastries. Salons de thé are normally open from breakfast through early evening, and they're likely to be filled during the mid-afternoon.

Bistros (sometimes spelled bistrots in French) are basically small restaurants, along the lines of a simple tavern or pub. Usually family-run, they normally offer a limited daily menu of home-style dishes.

Brasseries are large cafés with fairly extensive meal menus and daily specials. They usually open early and close late. The decor is often Art Deco. Many brasseries are associated with an Alsatian heritage. Alsace is an area on the French-German border that was shuttled back and forth between the two countries for many years. Most French beers are produced in Alsace. Early brasseries had a sort of dressed-up beer hall atmosphere. Some brasseries are gorgeous. We find brasseries to be the most versatile eating and drinking establishments. Many are now owned by chains, so it pays to be cautious.

Brasseries serve breakfast, lunch and dinner; have a wide assortment of offerings (far more than cafés or bistros; provide a convivial, café-like ambience (usually including some outside tables); are often quite beautiful yet more informal and more reasonably priced than a lot of restaurants.

Restaurants concentrate on food and beverages, without a café atmosphere. Medium-sized and larger restaurants offer a substantial menu (sometimes called a "carte")—often with a prix fixe option (also called a "formule" or "plat")—a few selections for each of several courses at a fixed price). Times vary by restaurant. Most operate at least from 8:00P to 10:00P; a few open up to an hour earlier and some close later—especially if they cater to the after-theatre crowd. Those that serve lunch generally do so from noon until 2:00 or 2:30P.

Several of our favorite Parisian eating and drinking places are described on pages 133-138.

Making Restaurant Reservations

Tip: You'll encounter a livelier ambiance if your meal begins around 9:00P or later. The French seldom dine before then.

Making reservations in French may gain you better treatment. You'll probably experience an exchange such as the following. Just follow the script. (**Y**=you, **R**= the restaurant spokesperson.)

Y "Je voudrais faire des réservations pour" (Zheh voo-DREH fehr deh ray-zehr-vah-see-OANH poor)... meaning "I'd like to make reservations for..."

...ce soir." (seuh swahr): this evening.
...demain soir." (deh-MANH swahr): tomorrow evening
...lundi soir." (luhn-DEE swahr): Monday evening
...mardi." (mahr-DEE): Tuesday
...mercredi." (mehr-creh-DEE: Wednesday
...jeudi."(zheuh-DEE): Thursday
...vendredi." (vahn-dreh DEE): Friday
...samedi." (Sahm-DEE): Saturday
...dimanche." (Dee-MAHNSH): Sunday
...lundi prochain." (luhn-DEE proah-SHENH)": next Monday

Making Restaurant Reservations (Continued)

R "A quelle heure?" (At what hour?)

Y "Huit heures" (Wheet euhr): Eight o'clock
"Huit heures et quart" (Wheet euhr eh kahr): 8:15
"Huit heures et demi" (Wheet euhr eh deh-MEE): 8:30
"Neuf heures moins le quart"
    (Nehv-euhr moah-ANGH leuh kahr"):8:45
"Neuf heures" (Nehv-euhr): 9:00
"Neuf heures et quart" (Nehv-euhr eh kahr): 9:15
"Neuf heures et demi" (Nehv-euhr et deh-MEE): 9:30
"Dix heures moins quinze" (Deez-euhr moah-ANGH kanhz): 9:45
"Dix heures" (Deez-euhr): 10:00

Tip: Parisians may opt to say the time in 24-hour terms (e.g. 2100 hours for 9:00P). If this happens, rather than dealing with an entirely new set of French terms, we suggest repeating the desired time as shown above and listening for confirmation.

R "Combien de personnes?" (or "De couverts")? (No. of people?)

Y "Un" (Anh) = 1   "Deux" (Deuh) = 2   "Trois" (Twah) = 3
"Quartre" (Kahtr) = 4   "Cinq" (Sank) = 5   "Six" (Sees) = 6

R "Quel nom?" (What name?) or "Votre nom?" (Your name?)

Y Say your last name, then spell it phonetically. (You may want to reference the phonetic alphabet on page 50 and write your last name phonetically below.)

_____

_____

_____

This used to be the point where you'd be asked if you wanted smoking or non-smoking. It's no longer relevant, as all Paris eating places are now non-smoking.

Making Restaurant Reservations (Continued)

R "Vos numeros?" (Your telephone number?)

Y You may want to write your phone number below, phonetically, so you can repeat it without hesitation; you'll find the phonetic pronunciations on pages 63-64. In Paris, phone numbers begin with 01 (shown in the first two spaces below), plus 8 digits.

" Zeh-ROH (0)" "Anh" (1)

_____ _____ _____ _____

_____ _____ _____ _____

R "Merci. Au revoir" (Thanks, good-bye) or "A bientôt" (Until later)

Y or "A ce soir" (Until this evening) or "A demain" (Until tomorrow)

Some Suggestions Once You're Dining:

- A waiter should be called "Monsieur" (M'SYEUH), meaning "sir," and NEVER "Garçon," meaning "Boy." A waitress is "Madame" (Mah-DAHM") regardless of age.

- Entrée (Ahnh-TRAY) means *appetizer*. A *plat* (plah) is the main course.

- "Je suis satisfait" (Zheu swee sah-tees-FEH) = I've had enough. (*NEVER* "Je suis plein," or full, as in "loaded.")

- L'addition, s'il vous plaît (Lah-dee-see-OHNH, see voo PLEH) = "Check please."

- The legal drinking age is 16, although enforcement is very light.

- Find a good book that provides definitions of menu terms. The best we've discovered may be difficult to locate, although we recently found used copies on Amazon.com: *The Taste of France* by Fay Sharman, published by Houghton-Mifflin in 1982 (but still current). *Marling Menu Master* is a serviceable substitute—currently available and much more compact.

- A prix fixe menu (also called "Le Menu" or "formule") means a fixed price for a multi-course dinner in which you usually have a small number of choices for each course. It's less expensive than à la carte (items ordered individually), as long as you can find items you like among the limited selections.

- When you order a meat dish:
  √ "Seignant" ("Senh-YAHNH"): rare (extremely rare)
  √ "A point" ("Ah pwangh"): medium (actually, medium rare)
  √ "Bien cuit" (Byangh KWEE"): well-done (on the medium side)

- To ask about available ice cream flavors: "Quels parfums de glace avez-vous?" ("Kell pahr-FUMH duh GLAHSS ah-vay VOO?")

- To ask for some ice: "Des glaçons, s'il vous plait." (Day glah-SONGH see voo pleh.")

- If you want something on the side, say, "à côté" ("ah koah-TAY").

- If you order water, say "de l'eau" (deh LOAH). They'll probably ask whether you want "gazeuse" (gah-ZEUZ, meaning sparkling) or either "non-gazeuse" or "nature" (nah-TEUR") meaning plain. Popular brands are "Badoit" ("Bah-DWAH") sparkling water and Evian ("Eh-vee-AHNH") plain water.

- A "carafe" of wine or water constitutes a liter; a demi ("deh-mee") is a half-liter, and a French "quart" ("kahrh") is a quarter of a liter.

Tip: The French don't keep a hand in the lap while eating. We've never asked why they don't, and they've never asked why we do.

Sightseeing and Attractions

Sightseeing in Paris can be both exhilarating and debilitating. We've already suggested that you do your most demanding sightseeing—walking, climbing, etc.—during morning hours when you're fresh. It pays to have an advance plan that considers proximity of attractions to one another and the best means of accessing each attraction. Don't worry about pre-planning lunch (unless you're in the mood for a picnic—see page 153) because lunch places are virtually everywhere.

The Advantage of an Initial Overview Tour

Some people benefit from taking a guided tour as an overview before forming a sightseeing strategy. Cityrama offers 90-minute bus tours with recorded commentary in 13 languages and covering most of the best-known attractions in Paris. They depart from (and return to) 2, rue des Pyramides (1st Arr., across from the Louvre) each day at 10A, 11:30A, and 2:30P. The cost is abou €23 per person. Children under 12 ride free. Tel. (0)1.44.55.61.00. Métro: Palais-Royal.

If you're willing to spend the money and can locate a driver who speaks your language, you may prefer a more informal and private tour of the city by taxi. This alternative means you'll see exactly what you request plus personal favorites of the driver—and at your own pace. Make a financial deal up-front, and do add a 15%-20% tip.

Tip: A taxi tour is more efficient when traffic is not at its peak.

Bateaux-Mouches ("bah-TOAH moosh), are tour boats on the Seine. Board at Pont (Bridge) de l'Alma. These "fly boats" (literal description) offer 75-minute cruises on the Seine, providing a river-level view of bridges and beautiful buildings (which are illuminated by the boat's spotlights at night).

Between April and September, trips leave each 30-45 minutes between 10:15A and 7P and every 20 minutes from7P to 11P. Between October and March, trips leave every 45-60 minutes from 11A to 9P, with frequency depending on when the boats fill up. The price is €10 for adults and €5 for children ages 4-13.

Luncheon cruises are offered each Saturday and Sunday at 1P (adults €50, children €25). Dinner cruises (jacket and tie) occur daily at 8:30P and last two hours (€95 or €135). Reserve for meals: (0)1.42.25.96.10 or www.bateaux-mouches.fr

The Batobus Shuttle Boat

Many of the main attractions are in close proximity to the River Seine. Accordingly, the Batobus shuttle boat can be a convenient way to get from point to point. See page 87 for details. Info: (0)8.25.05.01.01

Segway Tours

A unique tour involves the Segway—introduced to Paris in 2003. A segway looks like a scooter handlebar connected by a shaft to two wheels. The operator stands over the wheels and operates directional controls on the handlebars. It's motorless; you lean forward or backward to move ahead or in reverse An autogyro keeps the Segway upright and balanced.

Four-hour tours (incl. hour of instruction) are offered by City Segway Tours of Paris. Eiffel Tower, Les Invalides and Napoleon's Tomb, Louvre, Arc de Triomphe, Ecole Militaire, Rodin Museum, Place de la Concorde, Musée d'Orsay, Assemblée Nationale, La Madeleine.

Six people per tour. Year-round, tours begin at 9:30A, 2:00P and 6:30. Roughly €80 plus a refundable deposit. (0)1.56.58.10.54 http://www.viator.com/tours/Paris/Paris-City-Segway-Tour/d479-3588SEGWAY01

Paris Museum Pass provides free admission to more than 60 major museums and monuments (NOT the Eiffel Tower or Versailles) with **no waiting for entry**. You may choose to purchase in advance from http://en.parismuseumpass.com/ or in Paris at FNAC, Office of Tourism, tabac shops, museums and airports. €32 for two consecutive days, €48 for four consecutive days, €64 for five consecutive days.

Tip: If you don't want to buy the Paris Museum Pass but wish to avoid lines, you'll find that lines are shorter in the afternoon.

Sightseeing Efficiently

In preparing to explore Paris, it's a good idea to linger a little over your breakfast as you formulate a sightseeing "strategy" for the day. Sure, you'll deviate from your plan as you proceed; but start out by being as organized as possible. You'll save loads of time, conserve energy, and minimize the kinds of aggravation of which arguments are too often born.

Moreover, you won't want to be lugging all your information resources (like five books) around Paris. With a sightseeing plan in mind, you can take only the most relevant items with you.

In devising your sightseeing scheme, select sightseeing "targets" that form efficiently accessed geographic *clusters*. Make notes on routes, directions, and applicable Métro lines and Métro stations. Advance knowledge of the route to your sightseeing destination is far preferable to trying to figure it out on a map in the rain.

To assist in planning a geographically clustered sightseeing itinerary, we have developed six sightseeing *"modules,"* which are shown, beginning on the following page. Collectively, the six modules provide a cross-section of better- and lesser-known attractions. Four modules involve the Right Bank and the other two will take you to the Left Bank. Individually, each module contains sites that are in reasonably close proximity to one another. These modules may be a particularly useful resource for the traveler who will be in Paris for a relatively short period of time.

Each of the modules may be negotiated in a half day, although you may want to expand any of them (especially Clusters 4 and 5, which include the Louvre and Musée d'Orsay respectively). The first two modules should be attempted mainly in good weather; the next two are suited to mixed indoors/outdoors conditions; and the final two are less dependent on the weather. In general, we advise tackling the "good-weather" modules at the earliest opportunities, in case the weather turns bad toward the latter stages of your visit.

Module 1: "Art and Arc" (Right Bank—mostly outdoors)

Taxi to Montmartre (a huge hill and an arduous walk through a couple of questionable areas), instructing the driver to take you to the Place du Tertre ("Phahss dew TARE-truh" View Sacré Coeur Cathedral (see pages 122, 140-141) from within and without, and take in the incredible view of Paris. Explore shops, buy a Toulouse Lautrec poster, look for the Moulin (Windmill) de la Gallette (see pages 122, 140) and the last working vineyard in Paris. Have a drink at a café on Place du Tertre (where scores of artists ply their trade and exhibit their works). Check out the nearby Moulin Rouge nightclub (see pages 122, 141). You're going to be away from your laptop for a while, and there don't seem to be many cyber-cafés in this area; so maybe this would be an appropriate weekend foray.

There are usually taxis available at the top of Place du Tertre. **Taxi** to Etoile ("Eh-TWAHLL"), site of the Arc du Triomphe (see page 119) at one and of the Champs Elysées. "Etoile" means "star," and the Arc is at the confluence of 12 major avenues. If you happen to be in Paris on a state holiday, do this trip on that day, because a huge tricolor French flag will be flying inside the Arc. The top of the Arc has a panoramic view from Sacré Coeur to the Eiffel Tower. However, it's quite a climb, and the elevator sometimes doesn't run. A drink at a café along the Champs-Elysées affords great people-watching. But you should also watch yourself. If the cost of the drink doesn't fleece you, the pickpockets may (especially inside Métro stops in the area). Métro: Charles de Gaulle, George V, Franklin D. Roosevelt

Walk (or take the Métro) the length of the Champs-Elysées to the beautiful Place de la Concorde, where Marie Antoinette and numerous others lost their heads—literally (see page 120). Shop or visit a salon de thé (tea) on the nearby Rue de Rivoli. Métro: Concorde

Negotiating this module can be a little taxing and could take you a little further from your hotel than some of the others. You'd be wise to take some bottled water. Plan to find a lunch place with, among other attributes, good restrooms ("toilettes").

Module 2: "Latin and Literary" (Left Bank—mostly outdoors)

Walk through the beautiful, relaxing Luxembourg Garden (see pages 124, 155-156), where kiosks provide food and beverages for an al fresco snack. Consider a Sunday morning, when this place fittingly blooms with family activities among the bucolic beauty. Métro: Odéon.

It's now time to visit our single favorite section of Paris—the Latin Quarter—so named because various forms of Latin evolved into the official language of the university community at the Sorbonne until 1793.

Arrange to exit from the Jardin du Luxembourg onto Blvd. St.-Michel, and take at least a quick glance at the Sorbonne—if only for its history (see page 123). Walk from the Sorbonne to Musée de Cluny (perhaps the most underrated Paris museum, containing beautiful tapestries and Roman baths—see pages 123, 149). Continue down Blvd. St.-Michel to Place St.-Michel. Have a drink at St.-Séverin café (and you should return at night). We've never found a "watering hole" in Paris that equals the people-watching from a seat outside this café.

A little more than a block to the right of Blvd. St.-Michel (as you face the Seine), Shakespeare & Company is definitely worth a visit (see pages 123, 147-149). A little further in the same direction, you'll come to a park, in front of St.-Julien le Pauvre Church, containing the oldest tree in Paris (see page 123).

Cross either of two bridges (Pont au Double or Petit Pont) to Ile de la Cité—site of the Cathedrals of Notre Dame (see page 118) and Ste.-Chappelle (see pages 118, 139) with its unparalleled stained glass windows (a sunny day is best). Extend your walk to saunter around Ile St.-Louis, a quiet residential island in the Seine (see page 118).

Taxis and Métro stops are available throughout this walk, and it provides a fine opportunity for restaurant "menu-surfing." Since many of the locations in this module lie along or near the Seine, a day pass on the Batobus shuttle boat (see page 87) could be a useful transportation option. Métro near Notre Dame: Cité.

Module 3: "Pen and Then" (Right Bank—mixed indoors/outdoors)

Start by visiting Place de la Bastille (see pages 121, 139). The prison's gone now, but you can see its outline in the form of bricks in the street. The modern opera building is also here, although we feel the older Opéra Garnier (see pages 121, 144) is far more interesting and elegant.) Métro: Bastille

To catch some of the flavor of the "old" Right Bank, consider visiting Place des Vosges—the focal point of the venerable (now becoming trendy) Maris District (see page 145). Two very nice museums are nearby: Picasso and Carnivalet (see page 120), the latter of which chronicles the history of Paris).

End this module by visiting some of the 99 nineteenth century shopping arcades of Paris (see page 143), whether or not you buy anything. These are fascinating and often beautifully refurbished "passages"—predominately on the Right Bank—that used to house artisans but are now mainly filled with shops of many types. They are sometimes referred to as "the inner boulevards of Paris." If we were picking just one passage to visit, it would be the Passage Colbert, partly because Le Grand Colbert—a gorgeous throwback-design brasserie— may be reached from the passage. (See page134.)

Module 4: "Classic and Chic" (Right Bank—indoor/outdoor mix)

To observe chic in action, walk a few blocks on fashionable Rue St.-Honoré. Métro: Louvre, Palais-Royal, Tuileries, Madeleine.

Visit the Louvre (about two blocks from Rue St.-Honoré—see page 119). You'll never do more than scratch the surface in two or three hours, but try at least to hit highlights such as Winged Victory, Venus de Milo, and the Mona Lisa. The beautiful Tuileries Gardens are nearby. If panhandlers in long dresses approach and ask whether you speak English, look quizzical and keep shaking your head "No," without speaking. Métro: Louvre

Waiting lines for attractions such as the Louvre are generally shorter in the afternoon, which is a good time to experience this module.

Module 5: "Sights and Heights" (Left Bank—mostly indoors)

This is another good afternoon adventure. The Musée d'Orsay (see pages 124, 150-151) should not be missed. It is very manageable (far more so than the Louvre), yet houses a vast, eclectic collection of artwork, from French Impressionists to Rodin sculptures. The setting itself is a work of art—a beautifully preserved railroad station that was originally a palace in the 1800s. There's a very nice restaurant if you're there at lunch time. Métro: Solférino

Next, visit the Eiffel Tower, which needs no introduction (see page 124). Métro: Bir Hakeim, Trocadéro

Module 6: "Sales and Scales" (Right Bank—indoors)

If you aspire to major league shopping in Paris, two of the best-known department stores abut one another: Au Printemps and Galéries Lafayette (see pages 121, 126). Métro: Opéra

Nearby, the old Opéra de Paris Garnier is beautiful to behold outside and breathtaking inside. Now used primarily for ballets, it's our choice as *the most elegant place in Paris*. This place is incredible, and it's open for viewing. (See pages 121, 144)

Almost on the doorstep of the opera house, *Paris Story* is an excellent multi-media presentation tracing the history of Paris. (See pages 121, 141).

Comprehensive List of Attractions

Listings of both major and less major attractions follow. To the best of our ability, each entry is followed by the attraction that is physically closest to it. If you're designing your own sightseeing plan rather than using our clustered modules, just take this list with you and zip from one attraction to the next-closest one of interest to you. The general order of listings is east to west and south to north.

A thumbnail sketch of each attraction is shown, along with its location and (if relevant) hours of operation. Determine from the summary whether an attraction holds potential interest for you and obtain further details. For many of the selected entries, additional information is presented on pages of this book that are referenced in parentheses throughout the list. Alternatively, go to a conventional guidebook or make a phone call.

Ile de la Cité

Notre Dame Cathedral: Eastern tip of Ile de la Cité; (0)1.42.34.56.10   (Pg. 158)
  Mo-Fr 9:30A-6P; Sa-Su 9A-6P; tower view available to climbers   Métro: Cité
  May be most famous cathedral in the world, arguably the most enduring Paris icon

Ste.-Chappelle Cathedral: 2, blvd. du Palais; (0)1.53.73.78.50   Pg. 139)
  Daily, Mar-Oct 9:30A-6P; Nov-Feb 9A-5P   Métro: Cité, St.-Michel
  Cathedral on Ile de la Cité; view unbelievable stained glass windows from inside
  on sunny days; located behind the Conciergerie (below); classical concerts

Conciergerie: 1, quai de l'Horloge; (0)1.53.73.78.50
  Daily, Mar-Oct 9:30A-6P; Nov-Feb 9A-5P   Métro: Cité
  Riverfront Gothic-style royal palace from the 14th Century, later used as a prison
  and then a "holding tank" for guillotine victims during the French Revolution
  including Marie Antoinette, whose cell may be visited (along with the guillotine
  blade displayed beside it)

Pont Neuf: (spanning the Seine)   Métro: Pont Neuf, Cité
  Oldest Paris bridge; subject of many works of art and literature

Ile St.-Louis

Maison Berthillon: 31, rue St.-Louis-en-l'Ile; (0)1.43.54.31.61   (Pg. 22)
  We-Su 10A-8P   Métro: Pont-Marie
Famous ice cream/sorbet shop

Right Bank

1st Arrondissement (Les Halles / Tuileries District)

Forum des Halles: Rue Rambuteau and Blvd. de Sébastapol
  Former farmer's market; collection of shops, cafés   Métro: Les Halles

Bourse du Commerce: 2, rue de Viarmes; (0)1.45.08.35.00
  Mo-Fr 9A-6P   Métro: Les Halles
  Paris Commodities Exchange

Musée du Louvre: 9, rue de Rivoli near the Seine; (0)1.40.20.51.31   (Pg. 116)
  Mo, Th, Sa-Su 9A-6P; We, Fr 9A-10P   Métro: Palais Royal, Musée de Louvre
  Mona Lisa; Winged Victory; Venus de Milo; Pei Pyramid; mall underneath

Arc de Triomphe du Carrousel: Place du Carrousel   Métro: Palais Royal
  On axis with Louvre Pyramid, Pl. de la Concorde, Arc de Triomphe, La Défense

Jardin des Tuileries: west of the Louvre; (0)1.40.20.90.43   (Pg. 116)
  Beautiful former gardens of Palais des Tuileries   Métro: Tuileries

Palais Royal: Rue de Valois or Rue de Montpensier   Métro: Palais Royal
  Mo-Sa 9A-6P
  17th C. royal palace; beautiful gardens, courtyards; nice little shops on periphery

Comédie Française: 2, rue de Richelieu; (0)1.44.58.15.15   Métro: Palais Royal
  Nat'l Theatre, Molière and others since 1799   Mo-Sa 10A-6P

Musée de L'Orangerie: Place de la Concorde; (0)1.44.77.80.07
  9A-6P except Tuesdays   Métro: Concorde
  Monet's water lilies and numerous other 19th Century works

Musée du Jeu de Paume: Place de la Concorde; (0)1.47.03.12.50
  Tu 12N-9:0P; We-Fr 12N-7P; Sa-Su 10A-7P
  Contemporary art museum; former tennis court   Métro: Concorde

Place Vendôme: at the head of Rue de Castiglione; home of the Ritz and an
  obelisk topped by Napoleon depicted as Caesar; upscale boutiques
  Métro: Tuileries, Opéra

2nd Arrondissement

Galéries Colbert, Vivienne: 4-6, rue des Petits-Champs Métro: Bourse (Pg. 143)
  Renovated 19th C. shopping arcades; Le Grand Colbert is a gorgeous brasserie

Opéra Comique: 4, rue d'Amboise; (0)1.42.44.45.45 Métro: Richelieu-Drouot
  Mo-Sa 9A-9P; Su 11A-7P except July-August   Light opera, dance, plays

Right Bank (Continued)

3rd Arrondissement (Marais District

Musée Carnavalet: 23, rue de Sévigné; Métro St.-Paul   (Pg. 145)
Tu-Su 10A-5:15P   tel. (0)1.44.59.58.58
A museum dealing with the history of Paris

Musée Picasso: Hôtel Salé; 5, rue de Thorigny; (0)1.42.71.25.21   (Pg. 145)
Apr-Sep We-Mo 9:30A-6P; Oct-Mar We-Mo 9:30A-5:30P   Métro St.-Paul
Oct-Mar daily We-Mo 9:30A-5:30P; Apr-Sep daily 9:30A-6P
A major permanent Picasso exhibit in 17th-C. mansion (Hôtel Salé)

4th Arrondissement (Marais/Beaubourg/Hôtel de Ville District)

Pompidou Centre: 19, rue Beaubourg; (0)1.44.78.12.33
We-Mo 11A-10P   Métro: Rambuteau, Hôtel de Ville
Modern art center, contemporary architecture; excellent library

L'Hôtel de Ville: 4, Place Hôtel de Ville; (0)1.42.76.40.40 Tour leaves info desk at
29, rue de Rivoli 10:30A Mon.; phone (0)1.42.76.50.49 previous Fri. to confirm)
Ceremonial City Hall ; elaborate facade/interior   Métro: Hôtel de Ville

Bazaar de l'Hôtel de Ville (BHV): 14, r. du Temple; (0)1.42.74.90.00   (pg. 29,
158)
Mo-Tu, Th, Sa 9:30A-7P; We, Fr 9:30A-8:30P   Métro: Hotel de Ville, Bastille
No-frills value dept. store: home improvement, housewares, hardware

Place des Vosges: Rue des Francs Bourgeois and Rue de Béarin   (pg. 145)
Marais area; beautiful, historic square; shops, Victor Hugo house   Métro: St.-Paul

8th Arrondissement (Champs-Elysées District)

La Madeleine: Place de la Madeleine; (0)1.44.51.63.00
Mo-Sa 7:30A-7P; Su 8A-7P   Métro: Madeleine
1845 Greek-style cathedral with opulent interior; gourmet food shops nearby

Ave. des Champs-Elysées: Place de la Concorde to Arc de Triomphe (p. 22)
Best-known street; boutiques; U.S. fast food; cafés; tourists; traffic; set off by
gorgeous trees that are brilliantly lit near Christmas
(0)1.49.52.53.54   Métro: Ch. de Gaulle-Etoile; George V (Cinq)

Place de la Concorde: West end Rue de Rivoli, east end Champs Elysées
Historic square; site of 2,800 guillotinings, Luxor obelisk   Métro: Concorde

Grand Palais: 3, Avenue General Eisenhower   Métro: Champs Elysées Clemenceau
Largest ironwork and glass structure in the world; exhibition hall (0)1.44.13.17.17
Th-Mo 10A-8P; We 10A-10P

Petit Palais: Ave. Winston Churchill   Métro: Champs Elysées Clemenceau
Only courtyard and gardens open to visitors Th-Su 10A-5:40P   (0)1.42.65.12.73

Place de l'Alma: Cours la Reine and Avense New York   Métro: Alma Marceau
Memorials to Princess Diana, Maria Callas, French Resistance

Right Bank (Continued)

8th Arrondissement (Champs-Elysées District) - Continued

Musée Jacquemart André: 158, blvd. Haussman; (0)1.45.62.11.59   10A-6P daily
Beautiful art collection in magnificent private mansion; central staircase alone is
worth the visit; charming brunch/tearoom   Métro: Miromesnil

Arc de Triomphe: West end of Champs Elysées; (0)1.55.37.73.77   (Pg. 158)
Apr-Sep 10A-11P daily; Oct-Mar 10A-10:30P daily   Métro: Chas de Gaulle-Etoile
Iconic entry for victorious troops; roof view of 12-avenue intersection "star"
(etoile is the word for "star"); huge French flag flies inside arch on state holidays.

Parc Monceau: Blvd. de Courcelles; (0)1.47.63.88.60   Métro: Monceau
Rare plants, pagoda, Roman temple, medieval ruins, nearby mansions

9th Arrondissement (Opéra District)

Folies Bergères: 32, rue Richter; (0)1.44.79.98.60
Tu-Su Shows 7P (dinner), 9:15P (show)   Métro: Cadet
Oldest Paris music hall, famous for Can Can, feathers, breasts

Place Pigalle: Convergence of Rue Duperré and Rue Frochot
Famous for its bawdiness, sex clubs; little else   Métro: Pigalle

Opéra de Paris Garnier: 8, rue Scribe; (0)1.40.01.25.14   (pg. 144)
Daily 10A-5P for viewing   Call (0)1.40.01.80.52   for tours   Métro: Opéra
Lavish, elegant 1860 opera building; now primarily ballets; Chagall ceiling

Paris Story: 11 bis, rue Scribe; (0)1.42.66.62.06   Métro: Opéra, Chausée d'Anton
Paris multi-media presentation, narrated by "Victor Hugo"   Hrly 9A-7P   (P. 141)

Les Galéries Lafayette: 40, blvd. Haussman; (0)1.42.82.34.56
Mo-We, Fr, Sa 9:30A-8P; Th 9:30A-9P   Métro: Chausée d'Antin
Popular department store; luxury brands, affordable prices; ticket agency

Au Printemps: 64, blvd. Haussman; (0)1.42.82.50.00   Métro: Havre-Caumartin
Mo-We, Fr-Sa 9:35A-7P; Th 9:35A-10P Popular department store; pretty facade

10th Arrondissement

Canal St.-Martin: Seine from Pl. de la République to northern Paris   (Pg. 140)
Picturesque, old canal; numerous locks; walking path alongside   Métro: Bastille
Canauxrama boat trips: (0)1.42.39.15.00

11th Arrondissement

Place de la Bastille: Blvd. de la Bastille and Blvd. Richard Lenoir   (Pg. 139)
On-street brick pattern shows outline of prison where French Revolution began
Métro: Bastille

Musée Edith Piaf: 5, rue-du-Gast; (0)1.43.55.52.72   (Pg. 141)
Mon-Thurs 1P-6P; visits by appointment only   Métro: Ménlimontant
Former studio of Edith Piaf; contains many of her personal possessions

Right Bank (Continued)

16th Arrondissement (Chaillot District)

Palais de Chaillot: 17, pl du Trocadéro   Métro: Trocadéro
Museum of Natural History, Trocadéro Gardens, view of Eiffel Tower
(0)1.44.05.39.10   We-Mo 9:45A-5:15P

Musée Marmottan-Claude Monet: 2, r. Louis Boilly; (0)1.44.96.50.33   (Pg. 142)
Tu 11A-9P, We-Wu 11A-6P   Métro: La Muette
Old mansion; Monet water lilies, painting that spawned the term "impressionism"

18th Arrondissement (Montmartre District)

Moulin Rouge: 82, blvd. de Clichy; (0)1.53.09.82.82   Métro: Blanche
Daily 8P-2A   Windmill facade; Vegas-type revue; old Toulouse-Lautrec hangout

Montmartre: Métro: Abesses   (P. 140)
Major hill on outskirts of city; historic artists' enclave. Sacre Coeur on summit.

Basilique de Sacré Coeur: 35, rue de Chevalier de la Barre;
(0)1.53.41.89.00   Daily 6:45A-10:30P   Métro: Abbesses
Gleaming white cathedral on steep hill (Montmartre); visible at great distance;
view of Paris; dress reasonably tastefully

Place du Tertre: Square atop Montmartre; artists paint and sell their works   (Pg. 140)
Several restaurants and smaller eating/drinking places; souvenir and poster stores

Moulin de la Gallette: Rue Lépic and Rue Girardon   Métro: Abesses   (Pg. 140)
Windmill setting of famous Renoir painting; former mill, then dance hall, now a
restaurant with beautiful patio. Lunch, dinner daily 12N-10P

Marché aux Puces (Flea Market): Rue des Rosiers; St.-Ouen   (Pg. 143)
Sa-Mo 9A-7P   Métro: Porte de Clingancourt
Biggest flea market; 7 major pavilions; pickpockets abound.

19th Arrondissement

Parc des Buttes Chaumont: Rue Botzaris; (0)1.40.36.41.32
Daily 9a-sunset   Métro: Buttes-Chaumont, Botzaris
Large park with hills, boating, streams, waterfall, Roman-style temple

Parc de la Villette: 30, Avenue Carentin Carisa; (0)1.40.03.75.75
Mo-Sa 11A-4:30P   Métro: Porte de la Villette
Major park with science museum, music center, global-shaped cinema, gardens

Right Bank (Continued)

20th Arrondissement

Père LaChaise Cemetery: 16, rue du Repos; (0)1.40.71.75.60   (Pg. 141)
 Mid-Mar to Mid-Nov Mo-Fr 7:30A-6P, Sa 8:30A-6P, Su 9A-6P
 Mid-Nov to Mid-Mar Mo-Fr 8A-5:30P, Sa 8:30A-5:30P, Su 9A-5:30P
 "Residents" include Piaf, Chopin, Oscar Wilde, Balzac, Jim Morrison
 Métro: Père LaChaise

Left Bank

5th Arrondissement (Jardin des Plantes District/Latin Quarter)

Jardin des Plantes: 57, rue Cuvier; tel. (0)1.40.79.30.00   We-Mo 10A-5P (P. 156)
 Métro: Censier Daubenton, Gare d'Austerlitz, Place-Monge
 Huge, quiet gardens; Museum of Natural History; big zoo

Rue Mouffetard: Begins top of Rue du Cardinal Lemoine   (Pg. 150)
 Roman road; rich Bohemian history; famous outdoor mkt. since 1350;
 many interesting restaurants Métro: Place Monge

Panthéon: 19, Place du Panthéon; (0)1.43.54.32.95
 Apr-Sep 9:30A-6:30P Oct-Mar 10A-6P   Métro: Cardinal-Lemoine
 Crypt for notables (Voltaire, Hugo); city panorama from dome

St.-Julien-le-Pauvre: 79, rue Galande; (0)1.43.54.52.16   (Pg. 115)
 Daily 9A-1P and 3P-6:30P   Métro: St.-Michel
 12th C. church; courtyard setting for "Le Robinier": oldest tree in the city

Shakespeare & Company: 39, rue de la Bûcherie; (0)1.43.25.40.93   (Pg. 147)
 Mo-Fr 10A-11P; Sa-Su 11A-11P   Métro: St.-Michel
 Eclectic English-language bookstore; virtual memorial to Sylvia Beach and "Lost
 Generation"

 La Sorbonne: 47, rue des Ecoles; (0)1.40.46.22.11
 Mo-Sa 9a-6P   Métro: Cluny-La Sorbonne, Maubert-Mutualité
 Storied location of University of Paris; intellectual center of Paris for centuries

Musée de Cluny: 6, pl. Paul-Painlevé; (0)1.53.73.78.16   (Pg. 149)
 Wd-Mo 9:15A05:45P   Métro: Cluny
 Ancient building housing authentic Roman baths, beautiful tapestries

Place St.-Michel: At end of Blvd. St.-Michel near the Seine   (Pg. 146)
 Crossroads, melting pot, especially for young people; superb people-watching
 Métro: St.-Michel

Left Bank (Continued)

6th Arr. (Luxembourg/Odéon/St.-Germain-des-Prés District)

Jardin du Luxembourg; Access Rue de Vaugirard, Blvd. St.-Michel (Pg. 155)
(0)1.42.64.33.99   Open dly 7A summer, 8A winter; closes 1 hour before sunset
Beautiful gardens; model boat pool; jogging; view Sunday finery   Métro: Odéon
Odéon: Center of district is at Carréfour de l'Odéon   Métro Odéon
Primarily quiet residential area of historic literary heritage and theatre

St.-Germain-des-Prés: 3, place St.-Germain-des-Prés; (0)1.55.42.81.33
Mo-Sa 8A-7:45P; Su 9A-8P   Métro: St.-Germain des-Prés
Oldest Paris church (542) and one of the oldest belfries in France

Les Deux Magots: 6, St.-Germain-des-Prés; (0)1.45.48.55.25   (Pg.137)
Daily 8:30A-1:30P   Métro: St.-Germain des-Prés
Famed Hemingway hangout; fine people-watching even in poor weather

Café de Flore: 172, blvd. St.-Germain; (0)1.45.48.55.26   (Pg. 137)
Daily 7:30A-1:30A   Métro: St.-Germain des-Prés
Art Deco interior; floral exterior; literary roots; great toilets upstairs

St.-Sulpice: Place St.-Sulpice; (0)1.46.33.21.78   Métro: St.-Sulpice
1646 cathedral; beautiful columns and windows; Delacroix murals   8:30A-8P

7th Arr. (Eiffel Tower/Invalides/Sèvres-Bac District)

Le Bon Marché: 22, rue de Sèvres; (0)1.44.39.80.00 Métro:Sèvres-Babylone,Vaneau
Mo-We 10A-7:30P; Th 10A-9P; Fr 10A-8P; Sa 9:30A-8P   (Pg. 23)
Oldest dept. store; ceiling decor; upscale; epicérie (grocery) with gorgous displays

Musée d'Orsay: 1, rue de la Legion d'Honneur; (0)1.40.49.48.14   (P. 150)
Tu-We, Fr, Su 9:30A-6P; Fr-Su 9:30A-9:45P   Métro: Solférino
Impressive art collection; impressionists; impressive, converted train station

Les Egouts (Sewers): Place de la Resistance; (0)1.53.68.27.81 Métro: Alma Marceau
Tour of small part of sewer system and old pneumatic mail system Mo-Sa 9A-7P

Musée Rodin: 77, rue de Varenne; (0)1.44.18.61.10   Métro: Varenne   (Pg. 149)
19th C. sculptor's works; 8th C. mansion; garden restaurant   Tu-Su9:30A-4:45P

Hôtel des Invalides: 129, Rue de Grenelle; (0)1.45.55.37.70   (Pg. 151)
10A-6P Apr.-Sep., 10A-5P Oct.-Mar.   Métro: La Tour Maubourg, Varenne
Palatial home of Napoleon's tomb since 1840; war veterans' "hotel"

Eiffel Tower: Ave. Gustave Eiffel; (0)1.44.11.23.23 Métro: Bir   Hakeim,
Trocadéro
Daily 9A-12M Summer; 9:30A-11P Other months   (Pg. 158)
Completed 1889; three stages accessible via elevator; two very nice restaurants

Left Bank (Continued)

13th Arrondissement (Gobelins District)

La Manufacture des Gobelins: 42 ave. des Gobelins; (0)1.44.54.19.33
Tours Tu-Th 2P, 2:45P   Métro: Les Gobelins
Royal factory producing beautiful tapestries for 200 years

14th Arrondissement (Montparnasse District)

Parc Montsouris: Blvd. Jourdan   (0)1.46.63.08.09
Daily 8A-6P   Métro: Porte d'Orleans
Large, neat park; very natural; rolling landscape; lake; excellent restaurant

Catacombs: 1, Pl. Denfert-Rochereau; (0)1.43.22.47.63
Tu-Su 10A-4P   Métro: Denfert-Rochereau
180 miles of subterranean tunnels that house human bones but may be visited;
location of audacious WWII Resistance hideout/HQ; repository of millions of
ancient bones; underground street names mirror the streets above; movement afoot
to fill the Catacombs with cement

15th Arrondissement (Parc André Citreön District)

Tour (Tower) Montparnasse: Rue de l'Arrivée; (0)1.45.38.52.56   (pg. 159)
Not pretty, but very visible; 59th fl. observatory with excellent view
Daily 10:30A-7:30P
Métro: Montparnasse-Bienvenue

Eutelsat tethered hot air balloon: Parc André Citreön   (0)1.49.26.20.20
9A to 30 min. before park closes   Métro: Parc André Citroën, Balard
Rises 400+ feet; holds 30; Call first to check on weather feasibility.
(pg. 158)

Shopping in Paris

Terms on page 47 will help when you shop—especially in clarifying which floor is which in department stores. (Hint: The first floor is above street level.) Most department stores and upscale boutiques are on the Right Bank. The Left Bank contains one major department store and more moderately priced boutiques.

The major department stores are listed below:

Le Bon Marché: 22, rue de Sèvres; 7th Arr. (Left Bank exception; see page 124)   Tel.: (0)1.44.39.80.00   Métro: Sèvres-Babylone, Vaneau
Mo-We 10A-7:30P; Th 10A-9P; Fr 10A-8P; Sa 9:30A-8P

Les Galéries Lafayette: 40, blvd. Haussman; 8th Arr. (see page 121)
Tel.: (0)1.42.82.34.56   Métro: Chausée d'Antin
Hours: Mo-We, Fr, Sa 9:30A-8P; Th 9:30A-9P

Au Printemps: 64, blvd. Haussman; 8th Arrondissement (see page 121)
Tel. (0)1.42.82.50.00 Mo-We, Fr-Sa 9:35A-7P; Th 9:35A-10P
Métro: Havre-Caumartin

Two general merchandise stores that feature bargains are:

Bazaar de l'Hôtel de Ville (BHV): 14, rue du Temple; 4th Arr. (see pages 29, 120)
Tel.: (0)1.42.74.90.00
Mo-Tu, Th, Sa 9:30A-7P; We, Fr 9:30A-8:30Pf
Métro: Hotel de Ville

Monoprix/Prixunic/Uniprix
Tel.: 01.55.20.74.42 (headquarters)
Many locations in Paris (Check Paris Yellow Pages: "Les Pages Jaunes")
Discount clothes, pharmaceuticals, groceries

A good source of electronics, telephone equipment, adapters, music is:

FNAC (pronounced "Fnahk": 16 units around the city)
Check the Paris Yellow Pages (Les Pages Jaunes) for locations

Most upscale boutiques are in the 8th Arrondissement. Browse here:

Rue du Faubourg St.-Honoré (8th Arr.); Avenue Montaigne (8th Arr.); Avenue des Champs Elysées (8th Arr.); Place de la Madeleine (8th Arr.); Place Vendôme (1st Arr.)

Sally's Special Boutique Recommendations

Whereas Right Bank boutiques often feature chic brands of world renown, Left Bank boutiques tend to be more moderately priced and often contain apparel or accessories designed exclusively for the stores or even by the owners. Tasteful, interesting, reasonably priced boutiques are scattered around the Left Bank. Sally has found these places particularly appealing:

Petrusse

46, blvd. Raspail
7th Arrondissement
Tel. (0)1.42.22.36.28

Specializing in cashmeres, but carries many nice articles

Alain Figaret

Sally liked the one at 16, rue se Sèvres (7th Arr.): Tel. (0)1.42.22.03.40

Also at 21, rue de la Paix (2nd): (0)1.42.65.04.99

Also at 14 bis, rue Marbeuf (8th): (0)1.47.23.35.49

Also at 30, ave. F.D. Roosevelt (8th): (0)1.42.89.08.31

Also at 88, rue de Longchamp (16th): (0)1.47.27.66.81

Also at 134, rue de Wagram (17th): (0)1.44.15.14.04

Also at 18, place de Madelaine (8th): (0)1.40.06.94.90

Also located at Printemps Department Store (see page 121)

Wide range of apparel

Minute Papillon
34, rue Lecourbe
15th Arrondissement
Tel. (0)1.45.66.79.45

Jewelry, accessories, gifts

Don't forget to apply for your detaxé refund if you qualify. (See page 97.)

Synopsis: On the Town

• When making restaurant reservations, be armed to respond to the maître d's questions by referring to the scripted answers on pages 107-109.

• To avoid being overly conspicuous in restaurants, learn a few key French phrases (see suggestions beginning on pages 45-49) and dining tips presented on pages 109-110.

• Keep in mind the fact that the most famous attractions can be the tip of the sightseeing iceberg. In fact, many of the "secondary" and less commercialized alternatives, may be less crowded and more conducive to a meaningful bonding experience with Paris.

• Take a strategic view toward sightseeing activities. Develop a daily sightseeing plan that clusters attractions (at least by arrondissement) to make your sightseeing more efficient, less fatiguing, and less vulnerable to weather contingencies.

• Although shopping the grand department stores is a great adventure, you may find better bargains and more creative originals in small boutiques—especially owner-operated boutiques on the Left Bank.

Personal Recommendations

What follows is a gratuitous series of personal and very selective suggestions that might help to enhance your trip.

Dining Options

Eating places in Paris are smoke-free. A book describing French dishes (see page 170) should be your dining companion.

Elegant to Decadent

To ensure exceptional cuisine and elegance, pay an elite price (from €400 for two to considerably more). Consider lunch versions for less. Guidebooks list the "hottest" reputations, including such Michelin three-star restaurants as: Taillevent [8th Arr.; (0)1.44.95.15.01]; Le Meurice [1st; (0)1.44.58.10.15]; Guy Savoy [17th; (0)1.43.80.40.61]; Arpège [7th; (0)1.47.05.09.06]; L'Ambroisie [4th; (0)1.42.78.51.45].

Despite having only two Michelin stars, La Tour d'Argent [5th; (0)1.43.54.23.31] is highly regarded for its superb view of Notre Dame and its duck specialty, every order of which is numbered.

Frankly, if you have to ask about the prices of these places, it's probably best to avoid them.

Le Pré Catelan: Route de Suresnes (16th Arr.); (0)1.44.14.41.14

Our favorite three-star restaurant is a picturesque artist magne in the Bois (Forest) de Boulogne. The Pré Catelan consistently combines subtle elegance, gorgeous décor, elite service and excellent cuisine without being stuffy. The gardens are an enchanting luncheon option. This a perfect place for a celebratory dinner. It's been worth the main course price €71-€110 every time. Métro: Ave. Henri-Martin.

For a real "blowout" meal that will definitely impress for about half the price of the most elite places, we favor a couple of two-star restaurants that are elegant without being "stuffy," and must be considered absolutely world-class in terms of cuisine.

Restaurant Laurent: 41, ave. Gabriel (8th Arr.); (0)1.42.25.00.39

Understated elegance best describes this gorgeous pre-1842 building in a secluded location near the Champs Elysées. The food is exceptional (with a lot of little extras); the service is friendly yet efficient. An unforgettable place for special occasions. Try to sit on the terrace; but, if the weather's bad, the interior dining rooms are very nice. Main courses €60-€90. Prix fixe tasting menu @ €141 per person. Two Michelen stars. Métro: Champs-Elysées-Clemenceau

La Grande Cascade: Allée de Longchamp (16th Arr.):
(0)1.45.27.33.51

A major anniversary brought us to one of the most beautiful restaurants we've seen. Just have a taxi drive by this place, and you'll be tempted. Offset by a pool and waterfall (you can walk under the "cascade") and featuring an entrance created by Hector Guimard (designer of the Métro dragonfly entrances). We dined on the gorgeous terrace and enjoyed one of the best meals of our lives. Amazing food, wonderful little touches, unusually congenial service (they even walked us to our taxi). Main dishes €68-€72. Prix fixe menus €65-€185. Métro: Porte Maillot

Two ornate restaurants appeal more for the experience than the cuisine (although the food is very good). (No Michelin stars.)

Lapérouse: 51. quai Grand-Augustins (6th Arr); (0)1.43.26.68.04

This restaurant attracted us because of its unforgettable facade facing the Seine. Actually, the former 18th Century home has quite an intriguing history. One tale is that certain ladies of the evening, dining privately with gentlemen friends in one particular room, used to test the authenticity of gifted diamonds on the mirrors before they personally preempted the dessert course. Lo and behold, we were seated in that room; and the scratches were very much in evidence. The food and mystique were a compelling combination. Main courses @ €38-€70 and a prix fixe tasting menu @ €105. Métro: St.-Michel

Maxim's: 3, rue Royale (8th Arr.); (0)1.42.65.27.94   Métro: Concorde

We know, we know. Maxim's restaurant was famous long ago but is now somewhat of an afterthought. Yet we've had two such wonderful evenings that we wrote journals about the experiences. The place is plush almost to the point of decadence. The service is impeccable. Owned by Pierre Cardin, whose fine art collection is displayed on the third and fourth floors.

On our first visit, the waiter, who had once been a wine sommelier at Buckingham Palace, told us how the term "sommelier" originated. A traveling Lord of the manor would delegate a trusted servant to count the wine bottles each night in the master's absence, to deter other servants from theft. The French verb for "to total" is "sommer." Get it? Dick was certain he saw four World War II spies during that visit. There was one woman with hat brim slanted across her eyes....

Next time was even more fun, thanks largely to a wonderful pianist-singer (Michelle), who performed on the raised stage. She knew everything, from Dave Brubeck to Edith Piaf. Suddenly, at midnight, recorded disco music abruptly replaced her. Dick strode up to the Maître d' and protested loudly (in his best shot at French), whereupon they brought Michelle back for two more sets. We kept sending notes to her, requesting songs we knew would get the crowd going. Two of them were Piaf standards: *Milord* and then *Non, Je ne Regrette Rien*.

The audience began clapping in time with the first song. The place erupted in song during the second one. A little waif at the next table was wearing a flimsy bra and lacy shorts and having an excessively merry time; but, when she heard that song, she became deadly serious and quite emotional in her singing as though the song were a personal anthem. We like to think Edith would have loved it. We surely did.

We literally closed the place, leaving barely before the last employee handed us the key and departed. Just another little Parisian adventure.

Pricewise, your best bet is the prix fixe options @ €110 or €220.

And now, back to the world of economic reality.....

Except for special occasions, we try to eat dinner where we can get away with a budget (for two) of less than €100. The cost information quoted below is for price ranges of main dishes and prix fixe menus.

Our Number One "Tears-to-the-Eyes" Favorite

Brasserie Balzar: 49, rue des Ecoles (5th Arr.); (0)1.43.54.13.67
Métro: Cluny

If we had one night to live, we'd dine at Brasserie Balzar, which is famed for its literary heritage—in the shadow of the Sorbonne. The food, prepared the classic way, is quite good. We join many others in favoring the roast chicken, steak au poivre, or gratinée (onion soup). But one visits the Balzar largely to enjoy the traditional service and bustling atmosphere. Tables in the rear half offer a better chance of hearing French spoken around you. Banquettes offer the best vistas.

When the Balzar was bought by a chain in 1998, patrons held a strike to make sure no negative changes would occur. Read about it at: (http://www.newyorker.com/archive/1998/08/03/1998_08_03_039_TNY_LIBRY_0 00016065). Locals tend to be in attendance on Sunday evenings or for Saturday lunch. The English-speaking waiters are congenial but not patronizing. They patiently offer small language corrections for which Dick's grateful, and they're quite candid (if asked) about which menu selections they think are preferable. Main course items are priced from €18 to €35. From noon to 11:45P daily.

Belgian Beauty

Le Bouillon Racine: 3, rue Racine (6th Arr.) (0)1.44.32.15.60
Métro: Cluny

Le Bouillon Racine, on the outskirts of the Latin Quarter, is drop-dead gorgeous, with Art Nouveau decor both upstairs and down (although we generally prefer to dine on the street floor). This is actually a Belgian restaurant, with little touches to the cuisine that make it unique without being overly fussy or "suspicious." The selection of Belgian beers is substantial. Prices are fair too: €18-€21 for main courses and a €30 prix fixe dinner menu. Lunch and dinner daily.

A "Global Triumph" Brasserie

Le Grand Colbert: 4, rue Vivienne (2nd Arr.) (0)1.42.86.87.88
Métro: Bourse, Palais-Royal

A gorgeous 19th-Century-style brasserie that offers superb food and service. It was featured in the movie, "Something's Gotta Give," starring Diane Keaton and Jack Nicholson. We counted 98 Parisian light globes decorating the walls and center posts, which underscores the attention showered on the design of this treasure. We especially love the salade lentilles (with a touch of mustard). Lunch here if you're cruising the old Galérie Vivienne (see page 143). The best timing for dinner is after 10:30P (it's open until 1A) to catch the local after-theatre crowd rather than a majority of tourists. Reservations are definitely advised. Main course prices range from €18 to €31.

Bistros, Bistros, Bistros

Chez René: 14, blvd. St.-Germain (5th Arr.); (0)1.43.54.30.23
Métro: Cardinal Lemoine

The ambiance at Chez René is pleasant, and the cuisine exemplary—easily worth roughly €20---€30 for a main course. The Coq au Vin and Boeuf Bourginon are so beautifully flavored with wine sauce that we're salivating as we write this. We invariably wind up in conversation with "neighbors" here, as the atmosphere is quite congenial. There's a heated sidewalk terrace in good weather. Dinner Tuesday-Saturday. Lunch Tuesday-Friday. Métro: Cardinal Lemoine

La Petite Chaise: 36 rue de Grenelle (6th Arr.); (0)1.42.22.13.35
Métro: Sèvres-Babylone, Rue du Bac

Three sets of friends have independently told us this is their favorite bistro in Paris. The proprietor lays claim to being the oldest restaurant in Paris (1680). Varied cuisine changes daily, and the food is quite good. The street floor is a little more intimate (20 people), and the whole place holds only 70, so reservations are recommended. Open daily for lunch and dinner. Very French. Main courses @ €18.50; prix fixe menus @ €20, €26. Children's menu @ €12.50.

Allard: 41, rue St.-André des Arts (6th Arr.); (0)1.43 26.48.23
Métro Odéon or St.-Michel

A classic, old-time Bistro (from the 1930s), with dark wood paneling and a zinc bar. Open daily, it features classic, old-time cuisine such as coq au vin or goose. In the old days, you might have seen a celebrity or two here; but bistros have now proliferated to the point where they have to share the celebs. Main courses range in price from €19 to €39, and there is a €34 prix fixe menu. Lunch and dinner daily.

Lighter and Heavier

La Cigale Récamier: 4, rue Récamier (7th Arr.); (0)1.45.48.86.58
Métro: Sèvres-Babylone

Perfect place when your stomach needs a rest from rich food. Down a broad alley, removed from traffic's bustle. The specialties are melt-in-mouth, yolk-free soufflés as appetizers, main courses and desserts. They also serve some ordinary fare. A bit more convivial (including the service) inside than on the terrace. Reservations recommended. Noon to 11:00P except Sun. Main courses are priced at €20-€23.

L'Ambassade d'Auvergne: 2, rue du Grenier Saint-Lazare (3rd arron.) (0)1.42.72.31.22. Métro: Rambuteau

The Auvergne region of French is noted for robust food, with pork a favorite. Even the atmosphere of L'Ambassade (in the Marais District) seems solid, as you enter a bar with attractive heavy beams and country ambience. You'll normally encounter a congenial maître d' here. Unless one specifically requests to eat upstairs, they tend to seat non-French speakers in the bar, which is actually a rather pleasant dining option.

We often go for the beef or lamb, although we once had a veal/cherries special that was out of this world! If it doesn't come with your main course, consider a side order of aligot, which is a savory mixture of mashed potatoes and cantal cheese that's prepared at your table. Definitely make reservations. Main courses cost €15-23 with a prix fixe alternative @ €28. Lunch and dinner daily.

Dining in the Park

Pavillon Montsouris: 20, rue Gazan (14th arron.); (0)1.43.13.29.00
Métro: Porte d'Orleans

Located in the beautiful and peaceful Parc Montsouris (in the
Montparnasse District), where a nice walk might be in order before
dinner (during daylight) or after lunch. A nice terrace option in good
weather. Quite attractive and completely renovated a few years ago,
but we returned for the food. Classic varied French menu; prix fixe
dinner @ €51 (including one drink), plus children's menu @ €15.50.
Lunch and dinner. Closed Sun. Sep.-Easter. Reservations are advised.

<u>Venturing into Value Territory</u>

Crêmerie Polidor: 41, rue Monsieur-le-Prince (6th Arr.):
(0)1.43.26.95.34; Métro: Odéon, Luxembourg

Traditional French bistro dating back to 1845. Hemingway had some
of his moveable feasts here. Good home cooking. You'll probably
find yourself sitting at a noisy, long table with strangers. Main dishes
from €11 to €18. Prix fixe @ €22, €29. No credit cards. Located near
Luxembourg Garden. Lunch and dinner daily until 12:30A.

La Citrouille: 10, rue Gregoire-de-Tours (6th Arr.) (0)1.46.33.66.96
Métro: Odéon

La Citrouille means "The Pumpkin," as the orange sign will attest.
This is a little budget bistro on a side street just off our favorite walk
(see page 146). It's really nothing remarkable—just a nice clean place
with decent food and bargain prices, including an evening prix fixe
menu @ €12. Lunch and dinner. The toilet is not a major attraction.

Auberge de la Reine Blanche: 30, rue st.-Louis en l'Ile (4th Arr.)
(0)1.46.33.07.87

Bustling little family place on quiet Ile St.-Louis. Good food and
pleasant service at great prices. The menu is pretty basic, usually with
something for everyone. Prix fixe dinner @ €25.

Liquid Refreshment

We enjoy indulging in the occasional adult beverage; but it becomes something akin to an epiphany when we combine it with serious people-watching. Our favorite after-dinner spots are not cheap, but they're great vantage points:

- *Au St-Séverin*: 3, pl. St.-Michel (5th Arr.)   (0)1.43.54.19.36
Metro: St.-Michel

Our people-watching favorite. Dual charms of this café are the diversity of passers-by and the view of the St.-Michel fountain—an eclectic rendezvous site. One evening, an entire wedding party dashed by in full formal dress. Sit in exterior chairs bordering Rue de la Huchette and Rue de la Harpe to enjoy the best view of streets on which they sell everything from exceptional French fries ("steak frites") to lamb (shaved Greek style from spits). Ethereal moving shadows are cast on buildings along the Seine by Bâteaux Mouches tour boats as they pass. A taxi station (sometimes with very long lines late at night) is located around the corner.

- *Les Deux Magots*: 6, pl. St.-Germain-des-Prés (6th Arr.)
(0)1.45.48.55.25   Métro: St.-Germain-des-Prés

This is a famous 6th Arrondissement "literary café," closely linked with Hemingway, and featuring sufficient upscale passersby to make this an interesting "fashion show" in good weather The glassed-in front room (basically a sunroom) is a great refuge in bad weather. The name, "Les Deux Magots" ("Mah-goah") refers to two magistrates whose statues adorn a column on the ground floor. The hot chocolate is exceptional. There's a taxi stand across the street and a little to the right.

- *Café de Flore*: 172, blvd St-Germain (6th Arr.)   (0)1.45.48.55.26
Métro: St.-Germain-des-Prés

Located beside Les Deux Magots, Café de Flore has its own literary roots, being associated especially with Jean-Paul Sartre and Simone de Beauvoir. The facade is especially gorgeous. A nice upstairs anteroom is often deserted and adjoins particularly neat toilets.

- ***Café Mabillon***: 164, blvd. St.-Germain (6th Arr.)   (0)1.43.26.62.93

  The sheer amount of traffic in this part of the Odéon District makes for cosmopolitan people watching, but it's faster-paced, more touristy, and less interesting than the places on the previous page. But the coffee is better here.   Métro: Mabillon

- ***Au Sauvignon***: 80, rue des St.-Péres (7th Arr.)   (0)1.45.48.49.02

  This is our favorite wine bar, on the corner of Rue des St.-Péres and Rue de Sèvres. It's a great place to relax with a beverage or three about 4:30 on a nice weekday afternoon. Watch the Parisians on their way home from work, and think about your evening plans. If one isn't in the mood for wine or beer, they serve exceptional peach or apricot juice in small bottles.

On the Right bank, the Champs-Elysées has numerous options for sipping a drink and ogling the pedestrians on one of the most famous thoroughfares in the world. The Café de la Paix is a legendary place to meet for an apéritif (12, blvd. des Capucines, very near L'Opéra Garnier in the 9th Arrondissement).

However, we generally prefer to do our after-dinner imbibing on the Left Bank, where the people-watching is akin to attending a United Nations meeting. We reason that we can see a lot of Americans for free back in the U.S.; and the prices on the Right Bank are reflective of high real estate costs.

Attractions under the Radar

Naturally, all first-timers gravitate to the "biggies": Notre Dame; the Arc de Triomphe at the head of the Champs-Elysées; the Eiffel Tower; Sacré Coeur; the Louvre, etc. We love all of them, and they're included in our list of attractions beginning on page 118. However, we prefer to highlight selected attractions that may be somewhat overshadowed by the major Parisian icons. These too-frequently underrated alternatives are worthy of your attention and are less likely to be mobbed. Under each attraction, we'll refer you to the page that can furnish practical information such as telephone numbers and applicable Métro stations.

Right Bank

Ste.-Chappelle: 4, blvd. du Palais; Ile de la Cite

Sainte-Chappelle is almost literally in the shadow of Notre Dame on Ile de la Cité. This cathedral was built (1242-1248) to house Christ's Crown of Thorns and other artifacts of Christ's crucifixion (which now reside in Notre Dame). An architectural marvel at the time of its construction because it is bolstered by external buttresses. Sainte-Chappelle boasts an uninterrupted interior expanse that is mind-boggling. The sixteen, huge stained glass windows are absolutely breathtaking when viewed from the inside on a sunny day. Classical music concerts are held during evenings between March 15 and October. See page 118 for practical details on ste.-Chappelle. For information on concerts, telephone: 01-44-07-12-38.

Place de la Bastille/Canal St.-Martin: 10th/11th Arr.

For an infusion of history, consider visiting Place de la Bastille. Built in 1370, it was the King's prison that was stormed by French citizens on July 14, 1789, igniting the French Revolution. The prison was destroyed during the attack that freed the seven prisoners, so you'll be visiting only a memory. However, an outline of the original edifice—turrets and all—is formed by a pattern of bricks in the street at the intersection of café-dotted Rue St. Antoine and Blvd. Henri IV.

Not far from the site of the Bastille, the modern opera house at 120, rue de Lyon was dedicated on the 200th anniversary of the French Revolution (1987) and is open for viewing. We think its glassy walls resemble a vertical ice skating rink, but its architecture may be of interest to fans of modern styles. Most operas are now held here rather than at the original opera house.

While in the Place de la Bastille area, note the Canal St.-Martin, which begins at the Seine and travels north through a series of locks under the Place de la Bastille to Parc de La Villette—site of a large science center. A canal trip is interesting (though often chilly). A one-way boat excursion takes three hours. Call Canauxrama: (0)1.42.39.15.00. You can always make the return trip by taxi or Métro. A stroll alongside certain portions of the canal is an underrated Parisian pleasure. (See page 121 for practical details.)

Windmills and Vineyards: 18th Arr.

You'll surely want to visit Montmartre and Sacré Coeur Cathedral. After watching artists working and selling their creations in a hilltop square called "Place du Tertre," look for the two windmills that remain in Paris (of 30 which once existed). They are non-functioning but still of interest. The more famous, at nearby 79, rue Lépic, is what remains of a mill, built in 1640 and converted into a dance hall toward the middle of the 19th century. Renoir immortalized the dance hall in a gorgeous painting bearing the name *Le Moulin de la Gallette.* (A moulin is a windmill; a gallette was a sort of griddle cake.)

The 1876 Renoir masterpiece captures dancing and merriment in an extraordinary setting punctuated by the dappled sunlight shining through acacia plants onto straw hats. It's easy to see how this place was the essense of the Belle Epoque era. The windmill and dance hall have been gone for years, but a friend—a lifelong Parisian—recalls dances well into the 1950s. There's now an excellent restaurant in the Moulin de la Gallette. We've had wonderful lunches in the beautiful garden patio. See page 122 for practical details.

The other remaining windmill is visible from Place Jean-Baptiste-Clément at the top of Rue Lépic.

The last working vineyard in Paris is just down the hill from Sacré Coeur near the intersection of Rue des Saules and Rue St.-Vincent.

When you're ready to leave historic Sacré Coeur, look for the Funiculaire across the street. This venerable mechanical form of hill transport will take you down to a large children's carousel. Keep walking in the direction in which the Funiculaire took you, and turn right at the first major thoroughfare (Blvd. Rochechouart). Bear right on Blvd. de Clichy, and the Moulin Rouge with its red windmill sails will soon come into view—along with taxis and, eventually, a Métro station. (See page 122 for practical details)

This is the area where the famous—make that infamous—Place Pigalle is located. Take a gander if you wish, but beware of unsavory characters. By the way, it's ironic that the man for whom the now-seedy Place Pigalle was named was one of the foremost sculptors of the 19th Century. (See page 121 for practical details.)

Paris Story: 11 bis , rue scribe; 9th Arr.

This is a well-produced multimedia show about Paris through the years. In a theatre located near L'Opéra Garnier, shows begin every hour from 9:00A to 7:00P. The presentation is "narrated" by the image of Victor Hugo, and you can't do any better than that. You can listen in French or English. The price is €8 per adult and €5 per child. (See page 121 for practical details.)

Père-Lachaise Cemetery: 16, rue de Repos; 20th Arr.

The Cimetière Père LaChaise is a famous graveyard named for Louis XIV's confessor, Father LaChaise. This is the largest, most elite cemetery in Paris, with permanent tenants such as Balzac, Chopin, Maria Callas, Gertrude Stein, Jim Morrison of the rock group "The Doors" (of "Light My Fire" fame).

A map of grave sites is available at the main entrance (the second entrance from the Métro stop). The monuments are stately and majestic, with the possible exception of Jim Morrison's—usually a veritable trash heap of wine bottles and partially smoked joints. There were plans to move Jim to San Francisco a few years ago, but apparently someone decided to "light my fire" under the proper authorities, and the decision was reversed. See page 123 for practical details.

A nearby museum is dedicated to Edith Piaf at nearby 5, rue Crespin-du-Gast: Mon-Thurs 1P-6P—visits by appointment only. (See page 121 for detailed information.)

Passy and Musée Marmottan: 16th Arr.

The Passy district in the 16th Arrondissement, to the west of central Paris, is not a major tourist draw but is worth a visit. Belle Epoque buildings exude quiet elegance. On the western side of Pont de Grenelle (a bridge over the Seine leading to Passy) is a model of Bartholdi's Statue of Liberty, gifted by France to the U.S. and unveiled Oct. 28, 1886.

The Castel Béranger at 14, rue la Fontaine, is a beautiful Art Nouveau building designed by Hector Guimard, who was also the designer for the "dragonfly" motif that graces several Parisian Métro entrances. On the same street, at the corner of Rue Gros, is the beautiful Café Antoine—also designed by Guimard. At 47, rue Raynouard is Balzac's house, which may be visited (tel. (0)1.42.24.56.38).

At 2, rue Louis-Boilly is Musée Marmottan-Claude Monet, a relatively lesser-known museum gem in a 19th-Century town house, which is fascinating in its own right. The artistic highlight is a collection of Claude Monet's art—most notably 16 water lily canvases.

Also displayed are other works from the last years of Monet's life, including paintings such as *The Japanese Bridge* and *The Weeping Willow*, along with the famous *Rouen Cathedral*, and *Impression—Sunrise* (which spawned the term "Impressionist" and was both stolen and recovered a few years ago). (See page 122 for practical details.)

Passages (Historic Shopping Arcades)

Numerous covered passages were built in Paris early in the 19th Century and were occupied mainly by artisans. They have been renovated and are now shopping arcades (many quite beautiful).

There are 99 passages (pas-SAHZH). Our favorite is the gorgeous **Galérie Vivienne** at 6, rue des Petits-Champs in the 2nd Arrondissement. We particularly enjoy the beautiful Grand Café Colbert, a breathtaking brasserie with excellent cuisine (see page 134) that may be accessed from this passage. This arcade adjoins **Galérie Colbert**, which will take you to the street close to where you started. An interesting old book store is situated between the two arcades.

Galérie Vero-Dodat is also picturesque, although the stores may not be particularly interesting to some people. The entrance is at 19, rue Jean-Jacques-Rousseau, in the 1st Arrondissement.

Montmartre has three linked arcades (9th Arrondissement): Passage des Panoramas, Passage Jouffroy, and Passage Verdeau. These arcades are less ornate (even a little run down in places) but are probably a little more faithful to their roots. These three passages are clustered at numbers 10-12, blvd. Montmartre and 9, rue de la Grange Batelière.

Marketplaces

More than 70 open produce markets are scattered throughout every Paris arrondissement. Our favorites are on Rue Cler (Tu-Sa, Su morning—7th Arr.—pedestrians only); Blvd. Raspail (Tu-Sa 7A-2:30P, Su 9A-3P—totally organic—6th arr.), between Rue Cherche Midi, Rue de Rennes; and Rue Mouffetard (see page 123.) 5th Arr. Tu-Su a.m.

On Sat., Sun. and Mon., the 18th arrondissement flea market (Marché aux Puces) at Porte de Clignancourt-Saint-Ouen is large, fun, mostly under cover, and something to do on Sunday. It covers 75 acres (about the size of five football fields by three football fields, so wear comfortable shoes) and includes 2,500 to 3,000 stalls depending on which report one believes. (See page 122.)

This flea market is comprised of numerous market pavilions, including:

Biron: antiques, tapestries, tableware
Cambo: antiques
Dauphine (largest market): antiques, books, apparel
L'Entrepôt: very large items, from staircases to gates
Jules Vallée (oldest covered market): unusual second-hand items, e.g. posters
Malik: sportswear, trendy clothing, military surplus, leather
Michelet: Fashion apparel, accessories
Le Passage: furniture, clothing, books, curios
Paul Bert: Furniture, decorations, luggage, artwork, hardware
Rosiers: lighting, glasswork, lithographs
Serpette: antiques, art nouveau items from 19th and 20th centuries
Vernaison: furniture, textiles, paintings, toys, antiques, scientific weapons
Antica: paintings, porcelain, Chinese furniture

The market operates from dawn to dusk, and all stalls are open by 11:30 a.m. Early Saturday is the best time to find new items. Monday afternoon is the best time for bargaining. From the Métro (Porte de Clignancourt), walk under the overpass. Ignore the first few vendors of junk. The real flea market is centered on the Rue des Rosiers, the first diagonal street on your left, just after the overpass (as you're going from the Métro to the flea market). Be wary of pickpockets and sneak thieves. (See page 122 for practical details.)

L'Opéra Garnier: 8, rue Scribe; 9th Arr.

L'Opéra Garnier is "underrated" only by those who have never seen it. We feel it's the most elegant place in Paris. Most operas now take place in the relatively new (1989) opera house located in Place de la Bastille, while Monsieur Garnier's 1860 masterpiece—fictional home of the Phantom of the Opera—is now dedicated mainly to ballet. The new place is interesting in a nouveau architecture way; the old one is absolutely spectacular outside and beyond belief inside.

Take a guided or unguided tour. Feel like royalty as you ascend the marble grand staircase. Glide through the gilt-and-marble Grand Foyer. Enter the five-tiered auditorium and feel your breath catch. It's festooned with gold leaf and cherubims and crowned by a Chagall ceiling mural that pays homage to twelve operas.

Better yet, pick an evening when there's a performance. Wear something tasteful but not necessarily fancy (an open shirt and sport jacket for the man, a dress for the woman). Stand in line, starting about 6:15-6:30, to purchase from what is usually a good supply of last-minute returns from ticket agencies. They can be expensive; but we watched *Gizelle* from the fourth row, directly under the Phantom's chandelier, in plush red velvet *chairs* (no pop-up seats here). What a thrill!! (See page 121 for practical details.)

The Marais: 3rd and 4th Arr.

The **Marais** (or "wetland," which was drained in the 12th Century) has evolved from being a royal residence in the 17th century to decay and abandonment during the 18th and 19th centuries and to restoration, renovation, and revitalization from the 20th century forward.

The Marais serves to remind us that, although Paris is very old and Parisians have the reputation of being slow to change, the city is constantly going through a rebirth of one type or another. In the Marais, a sense of history blends with contemporary life to form an intriguing mixture, having evolved from a Jewish enclave to a cosmopolitan, "happening" area including a large gay population.

This district is the site of two noteworthy museums: Musée Carnavalet, dedicated to Parisian history (23, rue de Sévigné); and Musée Picasso (Hôtel de Salé; 5, rue de Thorigny). Musée Picasso, located in an old mansion, displays the evolution of certain Picasso works, depicting numerous intermediate stages. (See page 120 for practical details.)

The historical and aesthetic centerpiece of the Marais is Place des Vosges—an antiquated, stately square with a children's playground, shops, cafés and a top-drawer restaurant (L'Ambroisie). Victor Hugo's former home is identified by a plaque. Place des Vosges is located off Rue des Francs Bourgeois. (See page 120 for practical details.)

Left Bank

Our Favorite Little Walk: 5th and 6th Arr.

Flights usually arrive in Paris in the morning. After we've dropped our bags at the hotel (where the room may not yet be made up), we fortify ourselves with breakfast at our usual spot. We then embark on a walk we've been taking for years—the perfect reintroduction to our familiar Left Bank haunts. This jaunt may be completed in 20 minutes but usually takes longer because one encounters so many interesting diversions—a mixture of everything Parisian—shops, cafés, a cornucopia of people, an open-air market, antiquity.

Find your way to the intersection of Rue de Seine and Blvd. St.-Germain (6th Arr.), and turn left onto Rue de Seine. Continue to Rue de Buci (where cafés abound) and visit the small open-air market on the right. A few of the many restaurants in the area are quite good, but the food is mediocre at some of the overly commercialized, touristy places.

Continue on Rue de Buci to the Carrefour ("Crossroads") de Buci. Continue straight ahead onto Rue St.-André des Arts. About one block ahead on the right is a tiny cobblestone street called Cour du Commerce St.-André. This ancient alley is vintage Paris. The guillotine was invented at #9. Le Procope, reputed to be the world's oldest café (1686), is still in operation.

Returning to Rue St.-André des Arts, turn right and proceed until you reach Place St.-Michel, which we think is the crossroads of the Latin Quarter.

Find a crêpe stand (filled pancakes, hand-held like an ice cream cone) or stop at a café and do some people-watching. Our choice for the best people-watching is Café Au St.-Séverin (see page 137 for practical details), near the end of Blvd. St.-Michel, next to Rue de la Huchette. Return in the evening, and the people-watching will be even better.

For Dick, the walk is not complete without venturing down Rue de la Huchette (where there are all sorts of food vendors selling everything from lamb carved from huge skewers to ice cream to frites (French fries). We cross Rue St. Jacques to Rue de la Bûcherie, where Dick reassures himself that his beloved Shakespeare & Company (see description beginning below) is in good shape.

We are now officially ensconced in Paris; and we return to our hotel, where the room is ready for us to crash, and catch up on our sleep.

Shakespeare & Company and Sylvia Beach: 5th Arr.

This English-language bookstore near Place St.-Michel is a fascinating reincarnation of the bookstore/lending library established by one of Dick's heroes—a remarkable American expatriate named Sylvia Beach (to whom this book is dedicated). The daughter of a Presbyterian minister from Princeton, NJ, Sylvia visited Paris, fell in love with the city, and made it her permanent residence in 1916. She drove an ambulance for the French Red Cross during World War I— unheard of for a woman in those days, and an American expatriate at that.

In 1919, Sylvia established a lending library and bookstore, which she named *Shakespeare & Company*. For the next 22 years, she aided struggling young writers such as Ezra Pound, Archibald MacLeish, Thornton Wilder, Oscar Wilde, James Joyce, F. Scott Fitzgerald, Ernest Hemingway, and numerous others. Sylvia was like a literary mother hen, offering her "charges" encouragement, advice, sleeping quarters, and occasional doles from her meager funds. Historian Hugh Ford described her as "probably the best-known woman in Paris...certainly one of the important figures in contemporary letters...America's single most important literary outpost in Europe."

After a 1921 obscenity trial involving publication of Joyce's *Ulysses*, Sylvia bankrolled the project, courting scandal and bankruptcy. She nearly went blind typing the manuscript. Sylvia was tremendously loyal to Joyce even during the worst depths of his legal difficulties. Unfortunately, once the money started rolling in, Joyce was not good about reciprocating; and Sylvia recouped few of her heavy expenses on this literary milestone.

In 1941, Sylvia refused to sell a copy of Joyce's *Finnegan's Wake* to a German officer. Enraged, he promised to close the store. When he returned with reinforcements a few hours later, the bookstore had vanished. Sylvia and three friends had moved the 5,000 books and light fixtures up several flights of stairs to a place of safety and had even painted over the sign. She was later interned for several months in a German prison camp, where she became an activist on behalf of Jewish inmates. Upon her release, she returned to Paris to hide in an upstairs room on Boulevard St.-Michel until the end of the war, occasionally sneaking out to visit friends.

Sylvia never reopened the bookstore but remained a vital part of Parisian literary life until her 1962 death. The two locations of her store had been in the Odéon district of Paris (6th arrondissement)— first at 8, rue Dupuytren and later at nearby 12, rue de l'Odéon. At the latter location, a plaque commemorates the publication of Ulysses.

In, *Shakespeare & Company* (reprinted in 1991 by Bison Books), Sylvia describes a stirring incident during the Liberation of Paris. It doesn't get much more romantic than this:

> There was still a lot of shooting going on in the Rue de l'Odéon, and we were getting tired of it, when one day a string of jeeps came up the street and stopped in front of my house. I heard a deep voice calling, "Sylvia!" And everybody in the street took up the cry of "Sylvia!'
>
> "It's Hemingway!" cried Adrienne (Adrienne Monnier, a close friend). I flew downstairs; we met with a crash; he picked me up and swung me around and kissed me while people on the street and in the windows cheered.
>
> We went up to Adrienne's apartment and sat Hemingway down....in battle dress, grimy and bloody. A machine gun clanked on the floor.... We asked him if he could do something about the Nazi snipers on the rooftops.... He got his company out of the jeeps and took them up to the roof. We heard firing for the last time in the Rue de l'Odéon.
>
> Hemingway and his men came down again and rode off in their jeeps "to liberate," according to Hemingway, "the (wine) cellar at the Ritz."

In 1964, Bostonian George Whitman purchased half of Sylvia's books and founded his own Shakespeare & Company at 39, rue de la Bûchérie—near the Seine and Notre Dame. Not legally linked to the original, it certainly perpetuates the spirit of Sylvia Beach. Whitman claims he's a distant relation of Walt Whitman. He carries on Sylvia's practice of aiding fledgling writers, who exchange work for bed and food. He mentored us and even offered us free lodging during the writing of this book. The motto of the Tumbleweed Hotel (George thinks the people passing through are like tumbleweeds in the desert) is, "Be not inhospitable to strangers lest they be angels in disguise."

The cluttered, eclectic, eccentric store is at its liveliest during Sunday afternoon tea parties that welcome one and all. English is the primary language at these gatherings. Poetry readings are held on Monday evenings. There are wonderful views of Notre Dame from upstairs.

In 2002, George's daughter, Sylvia Beach Whitman, moved to Paris from England. She's gradually taking the reins from her 96-year-old dad so that Shakespeare & Company will persevere. She's about 30, and her dad is 96. Do the math! (See page 123 for practical details.)

Musée Rodin: 7th Arr.

At Musée Rodin ("Mew-zay Roah-DANGH"), beauty has many expressions in the works of Rodin—the preeminent 19th-Century sculptor of masterpieces such as *The Thinker* (which greets you as you enter) and *The Gates of Hell*. Rodin once lived in this elegant 18th-century mansion. The garden is a profusion of roses; consider lunch at the backyard garden restaurant. (See page 124 for practical details.)

Musée de Cluny: 5th Arr.

Musée de Cluny has the official name of Musée National du Moyen Age (Middle Ages)—Thermes de Cluny. This overlooked treasure is a former monks' quarters located atop Roman baths, built about 200 AD. The baths are huge underground rooms that may be visited and are awe-inspiring. Cluny also contains beautiful tapestries and an assortment of medieval artifacts, including carvings and stained glass. (See page 123 for practical details.)

Rue Mouffetard: 5th Arr.

One of the charms of Paris is its cultural diversity. Rue Mouffetard, which used to be a Roman road, is loaded with interesting shops and near-Eastern restaurants. We find this somewhat Bohemian area most appealing in balmy weather, when the crowds are out in force and the district pulsates to the rhythm of its own Parisian life form.

Exploring Mouffetard involves taking a taxi or walking up a gradual but lengthy hill and down the other side. From Blvd. St.-Germain, take Rue Monge to Rue Cardinal Lemoine (bearing right). When you reach Rue Mouffetard, bear left and keep going.

Not long after you reach Rue Mouffetard, a left onto Rue Ortolan will quickly bring you to a secondary market at Place Monge, open Wednesdays, Fridays and Sundays. Along with food items, this market dispenses household goods and jewelry.

Back on Rue Mouffetard, you'll almost immediately see the beginnings of the restaurants (French, Greek, Argentinian, etc.) and shops. At the bottom of the reverse slope of the hill is the very colorful and famous marketplace, which specializes in vegetables and fruits and has operated for several centuries. Operates Tue.-Sat., 10A-1P and 4P-7P and Sun. 10A-1P. (See page 123 for practical details.)

Musée d'Orsay: 7th Arr.

While the Louvre is the best-known Paris museum, we think Musée d'Orsay is far less daunting while containing a more selective but utterly compelling collection. Its physical beauty will appeal to you whether or not you are a museum devotee.

The structure was built between 1810 and 1838 as the Palais (Palace) d'Orsay. After an 1871 fire, the building languished in disheveled limbo until the end of the Century, when it was reconstructed into a railroad station that officially opened in 1900.

By the beginning of World War II, its train workload had been reduced to suburban service; and one plan called for converting the edifice to a hotel and sports complex with a vast swimming pool. During WWII, there were reports that some of the Parisian art spirited out of Paris by the Nazis traveled by rail from this station—which, if true, would be the height of irony, because some of that same art is very likely displayed now in the Musée d'Orsay.

After the war, the station became utilized less frequently for trains and eventually underwent a series of transformations to a rifle range; a parking garage; a public auction facility; a theatre. In the 1970s, the building barely escaped demolition that would have paved the way for a major hotel. In 1976, a proposal was approved for converting the building into a museum for French art of the years 1848-1914.

The Musée d'Orsay opened in 1986. It contains a staggering array of art objects, including our favorites—the French Impressionists such as Renoir and Monet. A huge clock that dominates the main lobby is mind-boggling; and a rather elegant restaurant may be found on the second floor. This museum simply should not be missed. (See page 124 for practical details.)

Hôtel des Invalides: 7th Arrondissement

The most popular designation of the Hôtel des Invalides (built 1671-1708) is "Les Invalides" ("Lays anh-vah-LEED"). A small area in the rear houses a dwindling number of old war veterans. It is also a museum, a venue for exhibitions and concerts, and most famously the resting place of Emperor Napoleon Bonaparte. His ornate casket is prominently displayed under a large dome whose exterior of gleaming gold leaf is visible from a distance.

Nineteen years after Napoleon's death, the British agreed to allow the return of his remains to France. The story is that, just before the body embarked on the voyage from St. Helena to Paris, the coffin was opened for two minutes. Witnesses swore the body was in perfect condition.

Dick possesses a faded letter written by an ancestor who fought for the Brigade of British Body Guards in the Battle of Waterloo that finally defeated Napoleon (whom the letter writer refers to as "Bonny"). The letter, written to the soldier's grandson, describes the battle and the annihilation of much of his unit. Accompanying the letter is an old Bible, which is missing the chapter of Genesis and has obviously been re-bound. The letter writer credits the Bible, which he had stored in his haversac, as stopping "grapeshot" intended for him.

There's a connection between Les Invalides and the 1789 storming of the Bastille prison, the event that triggered the French Revolution (see page 121). Prior to the attack, insurgents helped themselves to weapons from an armory at Les Invalides, after overpowering the guards.

The Museum of the Army is located on the site of Les Invalides.

(See page 124 for details.)

Public Parks, Gardens and Forests

Unfortunately, many Paris tourists are so intent on visiting monuments that they fail to stop and smell the roses (literally) in the more pastoral areas of Paris. In addition to two major forests, more than 400 public parks and gardens exist within the city limits—many of them charming spots for a **picnic lunch**. Ask at your hotel where to find a *traiteur* ("treh-TEUHR"), a store specializing in a variety of picnic-type foods. Buy some cheese, ham, bread, and wine or another beverage of choice—and you're all set for a picnic. (Don't forget a corkscrew!)

Bois de Boulogne: Just beyond 16th Arr.

The two forests (bois or "bwah") are located on the outskirts of the city—but they are technically in Paris. The better-known one is the Bois de Boulogne, located on the northwest edge of the 16th Arrondissement. It is said to be the second most-visited attraction in Paris (following the Eiffel Tower), but it's so spread out and diverse that it seldom seems crowded.

Just a few of the numerous features of the Bois de Boulogne:

- Longchamp Racetrack

- The very upscale and beautiful Pré Catelan Restaurant

- Shakespeare Garden by an open-air theatre

- Two other major gardens (Bagatelle and Rose)

- Bridle paths

- Numerous children's attractions (including a miniature zoo, bumper cars, a puppet show, camel rides and canal boat rides) at the Jardin d'Acclimatation (in the northwest corner of the Bois)

- Stade Roland-Garros—site of tennis' French Open during late May early June. Offers a variety of free activities year-round. Do not assume French Open tickets are unavailable; tickets are offered on many Internet sites. The official Roland-Garros site is at www.fft.fr/rolandgarros/fr/. (Click on "Billetterie." for information.)

There are many bicycle trails near the Jardin d'Acclimatation where one may take advantage of the many bicycle trails (often consisting of hard-packed soil with an occasional tree root protruding—so be careful). Consider renting from Paris Vélib. (See page 66 for practical details.)

Métro stations serving this area include Porte Maillot, Porte Dauphine, Porte d'Auteuil and Sablons.

Bois de Vincennes: Just beyond 12th Arr.

Just southeast of the 12th Arrondissement, the Bois de Vincennes was formerly a medieval royal hunting ground. The fact that it is secondary to the Bois de Boulogne as a recreation magnet for Parisians may have something to do with the fact that it seems less commercialized and more natural to us. Some key features:

• The Château (castle) de Vincennes (which contains a museum)

• The gorgeous floral park near the Château

• Two lakes

• An arboretum

• A "ménagerie," described by some as the best zoo in the Paris area and one of the largest in Europe, featuring giant pandas

• A lengthy ride for children on a small-scale train

We were blown away by the arboretum and gardens, which don't take a back seat even to Monet's Gardens in Giverny. The floral expanse is huge, and acre after acre after acre is just loaded with labeled plants indigenous to France and other countries throughout the world. The settings are beautiful, with streams and ponds scattered throughout what must be several square miles. Bicycle rentals are available, and are not a bad idea, although we really enjoyed walking—at least three miles. Take the Métro back to the main city, as taxis in this area are rare. The most convenient Métro station is Château de Vincennes.

It would be difficult to venture far in Paris without encountering a park or large garden. In addition to several smaller local parks, we have two larger favorites.

Jardin du Luxembourg: 6th Arr.

Located in the 6th Arrondissement is the Jardin du Luxembourg—the oldest public garden in Paris, and a stunning 60-acre gathering place for a mixture of Parisian gentry, exercise fanatics, children, etc.

Sunday morning is our favorite time here. Settle into wrought iron chairs near the 1625 Luxembourg Palace (to the north) that Marie de Médicis built after the death of her husband, King Henri IV. It now houses the French Senate and cannot be toured.

Delighted squeals come from the pool (south of the palace), where children and parents sail model boats (which may be rented). Church-attired Parisians stroll. Joggers jog. Birds forage. Tai Chi proponents martial their arts. Happiness and relaxation reign. All is well.

The Jardin is a no-admission site of many items of beauty, including numerous statues of noted women scattered throughout the grounds.

Some of the scenic highlights at the Jardin du Luxembourg include:

- Fontaine de Medicis, a fountain to the northeast
- Fontaine de l'Observertoire, a fountain to the south.
- A model of the Statue of Liberty by Bartholdi
- Public tennis courts
- Bowling courts
- To the southwest, marionette (guignol) shows (Wed. 3:15P, 4:30P; Sat./Sun. 11A, 3:15P, 4:30P) and Shetland pony rides for children
- An enclave of beehives

The Jardin is open between 7:15 and 9:00A, depending on the onset of daylight, and closes at dusk. The closest Métro station is Odéon.

Jardin des Plantes: 5th Arr.

The Jardin (garden) des Plantes is more of a huge park than just a garden. It's in the very busy 5th Arrondissement, but the city sounds don't seem to penetrate. Hours are roughly 7:30A-8:00P in summer and 7:30A-5:30P in winter.

Located here are:

• A floral "labyrinth"

• A tropical forest ("Jardin d'Hiver" or Winter Garden)

• A Museum of Natural History

• Greenhouses that are open from 1:00 to 5:00 except Tuesdays.

• France's oldest public zoo ("ménagerie") which has been described by some as run down, although we don't think so; in fact, its fun.

In 1826, the Pasha of Egypt gifted France's King Charles X with a giraffe, which was paraded through Paris before going to the ménagerie. Parisians instantly became crazy about giraffes. In an early example of fad marketing, giraffe images showed up on products of every description. Nonetheless, when Paris was later besieged by Prussians, starving citizens used the ménagerie as an exotic supermarket. (See page 123 for practical details.)

Nearby Métro stations include Jussieu and Austerlitz.

Paris under Cover (Inclement Weather)

What to do in Paris when it rains (as it often does)? Consider the following list of options, many of which have been noted previously:

- Visit L'Opéra Garnier (see pages 121,144)
- ˙ Check out the multimedia presentation on Paris titled "Paris Story" at 11 bis, rue Scribe in the 9th Arrondissement; (see pages 121,141)
- Go shopping at one of the major department stores or boutiques that are widespread (see pages 120, 121, 124, 126-127)
- Visit some refurbished old shopping passages (see page 143).
- Déhillerin is a "warehousy" fascinating store selling kitchen articles. Perfect for wedding gifts. We've gotten great values on beautiful copper pieces (which can be delivered to the U.S.—just make certain to get your tax refund as indicated on page 97.) Located at 18-20, rue Coquillère 1st Arrondissement: (0)1.42.36.54.80.
- Browse in Shakespeare & Company (see pages 123, 147-149).
- Tour Notre Dame (see page 118). (Try to save Sacré Coeur and Ste.-Chappelle for sunnier days.)
- View Napoleon's tomb at Les Invalides (see pages 124, 151-152).
- Investigate the Panthéon (see page 123).
- If it's evening, drop into a Jazz Club. Some suggestions:
  - √ Au Duc des Lombards; 42, rue Lombards (1st);
    (0)1.42.33.22.88   Métro: Châtelet, Les Halles
  - √ Sunset; 60, rue Lombards (1st);
    (0)1.40.26.46.60   Metro: Châtelet
  - √ Le Petit Journal St-Michel; 71, blvd. St.-Michel (5th):
    (0)1.43.26.28.59   Métro: Luxembourg, St.-Michel
  - √ Caveau de la Huchette; 5, rue de la Huchette (5th):
    (0)1.43.26.65.05   Métro: St.-Michel
  - √ Petit Journal Montparnasse; 13 r. du Comman't Mouchette (14th):
    (0)1.43.21.43.21.56.70   Métro: Montparnasse-Bienvenüe
  - √ Jazz Club Lionel Hampton; 81, blvd. Gouvion Saint Cyr (15th)
    (0)1.40.68.31.81   Métro: Abesses
- See an American movie. "VO" (Version Originale) means it's in English.
- Museums, museums!! Entry to the Louvre and Musée d'Orsay is free on the first Sunday of each month, but those days attract large crowds. Particularly underrated are Musée Marmottan-Claude Monet; Musée Edith Piaf, Musée de Cluny; Musée Rodin; Musée Jacquemart André; Musée Picasso; Musée Carnavalet, Musée de l'Orangerie and Musée de Jeu de Paume. (See pages 119 124 for details.)

Panoramic Views of Paris

The best multi-directional view of Paris is from the Eiffel Tower. For the elevator, adults pay about €4 to the first stage, €8 to the second stage, €11 to the top. Children about 60%. Avoid elevator expense (and long lines) by taking a private elevator to eat at the Jules Verne Restaurant (3rd stage—reservations essential—tel. (0)1.45.55.61.44) or less expensively at the less formal 58 Tour Eiffel (2nd stage—tel. (0)8.25.56.66.62). (See page 124 for practical details.)

The tower of Notre Dame affords a striking view of Paris to the West—just you and the gargoyles. Getting up there costs €7.50 and requires negotiating 387 stairs. (See page 118 for practical details.

The view from the roof of the Arc de Triomphe is spectacular, showcasing the Champs-Elysées, all the way to Sacré Coeur. If it's working (which doesn't always happen), take the elevator for €8 and avoid 200 steep stairs. ***Tip: Don't try to cross busy Etoile (the streets surrounding the Arc de Triomphe) on foot; take the underground passage.*** *(See page 119 for practical details.)*

The world's largest tethered hot air balloon (Eutelsat) ascends about 12 stories. The passenger price is €10 weekdays and €12 weekends. (Children receive discounts of approximately €3). Check on weather conditions before trekking to the takeoff point in André Citroën Park (15th Arr.) (See page 125 for practical details).

The free view of Paris from in front of Sacré Coeur Cathedral, on a major hill (Montmartre), is incredible. Hike to the dome for €5. (See page 122 for details.)

Some department stores offer fine views, including the self-service terrace restaurant on the roof of Printemps de la Maison (household annex of Le Printemps). Cafeteria le Rivoli, on the 5th floor of the BHV.), offers very good food and a nice (though more limited) view. (See pages 120 and 121 for practical details.)

The 59-story Tour Montparnasse is the tallest building in Paris (and ugly), but the view's pretty fine. If you don't want a drink up top, a trip to the observatory costs about €7. (See page 125 for practical details.)

During his first trip to Paris, Dick committed his all-time faux pas at the lounge up top of the Tour Montparnasse. Sally's parents were with us. At the time, the novice's perspective on French currency was that you spent a lot more francs than dollars for a given item, because the dollar was worth a number of francs. So he had gotten used to seeing many numbers on bills as the other three (who had visited Paris before) basically led him around by the nose and told him what to do.

But he had vowed—his very first Paris declaration of independence—that this would be different and he would take the lead. After we had ooed and awed at the views, the bill for our drinks came. "Have no fear, Dick is here," he announced, pulling out his trusty American Express Card and stifling his companions' protests with a benevolent wave of the hand that would have done Casey at the Bat proud.

They ran the Amex Card and brought the total bill. Dick blithely signed the check and added a 20% tip. (Darned if his father-in-law would get the impression that their daughter's new husband was a cheapskate.) Dick noticed smiles playing on their faces and felt his generosity had hit home. What he didn't know was that they were well aware that almost all beverage and meal bills in France already have a 15% gratuity added.

The waiter collected the bill and bustled away, as we prepared to leave. Suddenly he came running back with a very pale face, pointing to the signed check and jabbering words that only Sally had a shot at understanding. She listened, and turned to Dick. "Remember how you've been saying it's weird to see so many numbers in the cost of everything here?" "Sure, but I'm used to it now," he replied brashly.

"Well, buddy, you just added your 20% tip to the **date** and totaled it." Meanwhile, Dick's in-laws were stuffing their mouths with everything that wasn't tied down, as they realized Dick had tipped several thousand dollars. Some alarm at Amex had saved his bacon.

Excursions from Paris

Modes of Travel

In case you should get the urge to expand your geographic horizons in France, we have a few suggestions. We've done it by air (obviously the fastest option; but air travel within Europe can be very expensive), train (the smoothest and most hassle-free means) and rented car (the most flexible alternative, but be aware of the whopping tax).

Automobile Travel

- You may be better off renting a car before you leave home. But, if you have a need while in Paris, the following car-rental telephone numbers may be called toll-free from anywhere in France:

Avis	08.20.05.05.05
Hertz	08.25.88.97.55
Budget	08.25.00.35.64
Europecar	08.25.35.83.58

- A U.S. driver's license will suffice to rent a car in France.

- Seat belts are mandatory in France, and they drive on the right side.

Train Travel

- TVG trains will whisk you away at 150-200 MPH. Be prepared for a little vibration if you attempt to write while aboard.

- Information windows at a train station (or gare, pronounced "gahr") can tell you about package deals for taking a train and then renting either a car or a bicycle upon reaching your destination.

- The S.N.C.F. operates long-distance ("Grandes Lignes") trains from six stations in Paris:

  Gare du Nord (for travel northeast toward Germany)
  Gare de l'est (for travel southeast toward Germany)
  Gare de Lyon (for travel southwest toward Lyon, France)
  Gare d'Austerlitz (for travel southwest toward Spain)
  Gare St.-Lazarre (for travel west toward Rouen, France)
  Gare Montparnasse (for travel south toward Nantes, France)

- Toll-free telephone information for S.N.C.F. (may be dialed from anywhere in France): 08.36.35.35.35

Some Recommended Side Trips

There are so many possible side trips from Paris that it would not be in keeping with the digest philosophy of this book to try to include all of them. We've chosen to list a few that we feel are particularly worthy of attention. We've omitted others such as Versailles, which we found to be beautiful but more appropriate for a relatively brief stop than an overnight.

Provence

Many guidebooks are devoted to Provence, which is in the South of France and is invariably warmer than Paris. Provence offers a host of options for sites to visit, depending on whether you want history, beauty, relaxation, countryside, beaches, farms, canals, walled cities— whatever.

Aix-en-Provence ("Eks") is our favorite place in Provence. It's enough of a city (in some ways a miniature Paris) to offer plenty of resources, yet sufficiently country-like to satisfy one's pastoral urges. A university town, it contains a mixture of residents—from artisans and shopkeepers to students from all over the world. There are numerous art galleries, and Aix is famed for its tapestry museum. A major music festival is held from mid-July through mid-August, with concerts in a palace courtyard.

The requisite cathedral contains artifacts of the city from as far back as the 5th Century. And, how about a museum of natural history that displays unhatched dinosaur eggs? A vast honey comb of small shops winds through the oldest part of the city ("Vieux Aix"). It's difficult not to become lost in this maze.

The Cours Mirabeau is the main thoroughfare of the city—named after the Count of Mirabeau, a scandalous politician during the French Revolution. In the middle of the Cours Mirabeau is the Fontaine d'Eau Chaude—a warm-water fountain covered with moss. The water comes from hot springs that were used by the Romans. The cafés along the Cours provide an ideal setting for fascinating people-watching.

Elsewhere in Provence, Avignon is a charming city that houses the Papal Palace from the 14th Century. Also, in the eastern sector of Provence lies a huge gorge with the nickname "The Grand Canyon of Verdon." Actually, it's the height to which you drive as much as the depth of the canyon that makes the view spectacular.

Champagne Country

A drive through wine country to the northeast of Paris is relaxing, scenic and instructive. Along with vineyard tours (we particularly enjoyed the Moët tour in the town of Epernay), the town of Reims ("Ranhs") deserves attention. Nearly leveled during World War II, Reims ironically became the site of Nazi German's unconditional surrender on May 7, 1945, in General Eisenhower's war room, which (with war maps still up on the walls) is now part of the Musée de la Reddition (Surrender Museum), located at 12, rue Franklin Roosevelt.

The Loire Valley

The Loire Valley (best reached by car) contains a wide variety of fascinating châteaux (castles). Many have interesting sound-and-light shows in the evenings during warm-weather months.

Our favorite château is the beautiful Chenonceau in the town of Chenonceaux. Spanning the peaceful River Cher, Chenonceau has dazzling gardens and an intriguing past. Much of its history involves Catherine de Médicis and how she got rid of her husband's in-house mistress, Diane de Poitiers, by giving Diane another château (Chaumont) as a sort of consolation prize. The architecture of Chenenceau, bearing the imprints of both women, is fascinating.

Auberge du Le Bon Laboreur is a very nice hotel with a superior restaurant. It's very close to the chateau. Rooms rates are priced as low as €120. http://www.bonlaboureur.com/RestauUK.asp

Giverny and Monet's Gardens

The artist Claude Monet's house and gardens in Giverny (an easy 45-mile train ride northwest of Paris in Normandy) are inspiring. Nearly half a million people visit in a typical year.

In 1883, Monet, his two sons by his late wife Camille, his mistress (Alice Hoschedé), and her six children from a previous marriage all moved to this little village midway between Paris and Rouen. It was here that Monet was inspired to create works such as his *Nymphéas* series and *The Lily Pond* (1899-1906).

Many consider the botanical gardens that he laid out to be Monet's greatest masterpiece. The various months of the year are represented through different colorations. Monet's Japanese print collection remains on the walls of his home, which may be toured. Monet's studio, in a separate building, may also be visited.

Seven years after moving to Giverny, Monet bought land across the road. He diverted a stream and built a pool, which became the setting for the water lilies featured in many of his paintings. A weeping willow, bamboo, wisteria, azaleas and a Japanese bridge are prominent.

In 1992, an American Museum was established in Giverny. Its goal is to demonstrate how French and American impressionists influenced one another.

Giverny is about 3.5 miles inland from the town of Vernon, where one disembarks if traveling by water or rail (from Gare St.-Lazare in Paris on the Rouen train—roughly €25 round trip). The most popular ways of getting from town to the Monet property are taxi and a bus, which meets each train from Paris. It's also a picturesque walk or bicycle ride (bikes may be rented at the train station), although the Vernon-Giverny road is frequented by a fair amount of fast traffic.

The gardens and house are open from April through October except Mondays and holidays. The best time to visit is May or June, when the rhododendrons and wisteria are in full bloom and the crowds are less constricting than during summer months. The gardens are open 10A to 6P. The house is open 10A-noon and 2P-6P. Admission is €4 to see the gardens and €6 if you also want to venture into Monet's house.

Number One Recommended Side Trip—Echoes of Heroes

So, given all of the available options, what would be our number one recommendation for a side trip from Paris? There's absolutely no question. **You must visit the American Cemetery and Omaha Beach in Normandy. Just do it! Drive...take a train...hitchhike if necessary. But don't miss the opportunity.**

The cemetery is actually on American soil—a gift from France—on a plateau situated above Omaha Beach (which was the site of the great majority of deaths during the Normandy Invasion). We always begin by becoming "reacquainted" with row upon row of the 9,387 permanent residents. Then we stand at the top of the bluffs, noting the highly protected German bunkers that still overlook the fully exposed landing beach. Next, we descend to the edge of the water and stare up at the dominating hills, as we try to imagine what it was like for the first assault wave. Finally, we visit nearby Pointe du Hoc and peer straight down the cliff walls that were scaled by American Rangers in the face of a German machine gun emplacement at the top.

The entire experience always has a dramatic impact on us. Above all else, it provides an important perspective from which to reflect on the myriad aspects of life that so often seem challenging but—in comparison—are really quite trivial.

We are most proud to have attended the 40th anniversary of D-Day in 1984. In Paris, we rented an old blue van, in which we stashed a couple of bicycles we had purchased (later to be shipped home). Determined to drive as far as the authorities would allow and bike the rest of the way, we eventually were astounded to discover our beat-up van in the middle of a U.S. Army convoy as we neared Omaha Beach. We drove right down onto the beach, as crowds lining the streets waved flags and yelled, "Libérateurs, Libérateurs."

We witnessed a mock invasion from the beach and then went up to the American Cemetery, which we found to be closed to all except approximately 2,500 invited VIPs and dignitaries who were slated to attend a ceremony to be held at the D-Day Memorial, in front of a long reflecting pool. We were assured that entry was out of the question.

On an impulse, Dick knocked on the door of a nearby trailer and found an American woman, in charge of logistics, standing alone among a sea of huge cartons. Dick pleaded for entry to the ceremonies until she said, "I'm sorry, but I can't begin to address your plight until all these boxes are moved over there" (gesturing to a distant point).

"Say no more," Dick responded. In a few minutes, every container was relocated, and we were passing through the metal detectors—surrounded by veterans who were discussing their D-Day adventures and comparing war memorabilia. Our ribbon-bedecked entry badges now hang proudly in our bedroom and will always serve as reminders of the incredibly moving ceremony featuring speeches by the American and French presidents. You may see Ronald Reagan delivering his moving speech at: http://thetension.blogspot.com/2009/06/flashback-video-president-reagans.html

Omaha Beach is in Colleville-sur-Mer. It's possible to do a round trip by train from and to Paris in one very long day. Trains run to nearby Bayeux from Gare St.-Lazare in Paris (about a three-hour trip). If you go by train, there are only a couple of taxis (which are often busy taking children to and from school)—and no car rental agencies—near the Bayeux train station. Thus it's highly advisable to take a tour of the landing beaches. Several tour options are offered by Viator.
http://www.viator.com/Bayeux-attractions/Omaha-Beachtourstickets/d909-a1634

It's a 170—mile, one-way automobile trip from Paris: Route A-13 to Caen, then N-13 to Bayeux and Formigny, then D-517 to St.-Laurent-sur-Mer, then D-514 to Colleville-sur-Mer. Plan to stay overnight.

We were so inspired by our D-Day experience that we returned to France two months later for the 40th anniversary celebration of the Liberation of Paris (see pages 42-43 for that tale).

There could be no better way of renewing one's commitment to U.S. citizenship than to pass in review of the silent heroes whose visit in terror to France paved the way for those who follow to visit in peace.

Reference Material

Here are the best references we have found on Paris, in no particular order. Some were most recently published a few years ago, but Paris is relatively slow to change, and we feel the basic quality of a reference should be the main priority. Most are available on Amazon.

Paris par Arrondissement et Communes de Banlieue
- Detailed map by arrondissement, including Métro stations, plus overview map
- Alphabetical listing of every street in Paris; list of all bus stops
- Compact; updated periodically, last in 2008; a "must" for many Parisians and us

DK Eyewitness Travel Guides: Paris, Tiller (DK Travel)
- Detailed compilation of Paris attractions, restaurants, etc.; filled with photos
- Updated periodically, most recently in 2010

Frommer's Paris, Porter and Price (Published by Frommer's)
- Long-time, comprehensive, conventional guide book; many color photos
- Published each year, most recently for 2011

Access Paris, Richard Saul Wurman (Access Press)
- Descriptions of things to see and do; many suggestions are off the beaten track
- Updated periodically, most recently in 2008

Pariswalks, Landes and Landes (Henry Holt & Company)
- Several detailed Paris walks, maps can lead to discovery, adventure and insight
- Updated periodically, most recently in 2005

Hotels of Character and Charm in Paris, Tatiana de Beaumont (Hunter)
- Describes more than 200 small hotels in detail
- Updated periodically, most recently in 2001

Hungry for Paris, Alexander Lobrando (Random House)

- In-depth insights on 100 selected eating places in Paris, 2007
- Excellent detail on background, cuisines and dining experiences

Special Places to Stay (Paris Hotels), Alastair Sawday (Sawday), 2007

- Reviews of 111 very good medium- and smaller-sized Paris hotels
- Emphasizes the "feel" of hotels as well as practical details

Great Eats Paris, Sandra A. Gustafson (Chronicle Books)
Great Sleeps Paris, Sandra A. Gustafson (Chronicle Books)
- Describe many eating, sleeping places respectively, with emphasis on value
- Updated periodically, both most recently in 2007

The Taste of France: 25th Anniv. Ed., Adrian Bailey et al. (Stewart, Tabori, Chang)
- The bible for defining French menu terms in English
- 25th anniversary edition (hardcover), 2007; earlier softcover copies on Amazon

The Marling Menu-Master for France, Marling and Marling (Altarinda Books)
- Compact menu translations from French to English; not updated since 1971
- Much less comprehensive than *The Taste of France* but tiny and easy to carry

Notes

Notes

Index